KU-657-932

Hymns of Faith & Freedom

THE CHALICE PRESS
London

Published with the authority of
the General Synod of the Non-Subscribing
Presbyterian Church of Ireland

First edition published by the Chalice Press, 1991

117 Mansford Street, Bethnal Green, London E2 6LX

Designed by Jacky Wedgwood

Phototypesetting by
Church Action with the Unemployed and
Computape (Pickering) Ltd, North Yorkshire

Printed by Hartnolls Ltd, Bodmin, Cornwall

ISBN 1 873014 00 7

Contents

(For a more precise or specific choice of hymns, readers are advised to consult the Index of Themes under the appropriate sections)

Preface

THIS BOOK is a radical revision of *Hymns of Worship* (revised), published by Lindsey Press in 1962. We hope it will serve a double purpose: as a collection large enough in itself to serve as a hymn book for congregations in our community of churches and as a supplementary book for those who have *Hymns for Living* (Lindsey Press 1985), but find it in certain respects inadequate for their worship needs. The liberal Christian character of *Hymns of Faith & Freedom* will be apparent on even the most cursory of inspections. It was our deliberate intent to give it such a character.

We regret that financial considerations must delay the issuing of an accompanying tune book, but not, we trust, for long. Meanwhile it should be possible to use the vast majority of the hymns in this book with the purchase of one additional hymnal: *Hymns & Psalms* (Methodist Publishing House). This is an excellent book and readily available. Throughout *Hymns of Faith & Freedom* we have suggested accessible tunes and the tune index will indicate their sources.

No hymn book could ever hope to meet with unanimous approval. Some worshippers find their favourite hymns omitted and others disapprove of the inclusions. Some hymns we had hoped to include, we were denied permission to use. Some lyrics were included, not because they were of superlative quality, but because our congregations would expect to find them here. Others were excluded despite pleas by one or other of us on the working-party. There are a number of criteria which determine selection or exclusion, but the Benthamite principle of giving the greatest happiness to the greatest number of hymn singers in our community of churches is not a safe or sure one.

Our fundamental aim in compilation is well expressed in N.P. Goldhawk's *On Hymns and Hymn Books*, page 88 (Epworth Press 1979):

"While reflecting to a degree the religious temper of the age in which it is produced, and giving due expression to new insights and a forward-looking point of view, it must at the same time do justice to the great traditional emphasis and ethos of the denomination – no easy requirements."

Although *Hymns of Faith & Freedom* is not an 'official' denominational book, it is meant to serve the worship needs of a particular liberal Christian constituency. Consequently, while we have drawn the majority of our lyrics from our traditional sources, we have taken this opportunity to bring into the repertoire some of the best contemporary hymns, a very few totally new ones and some lyrics which appeared in earlier collections and had subsequently for a variety of reasons been excluded or had never been accepted.

To determine our selection, we have asked ourselves a few basic questions: has this lyric sufficient literary merit? Is it so germane to our tradition that it must be included? Does it supply a real need in our public worship? And, above all, when questions of theology or christology have been involved: is this expression of devotion truly scriptural? That is a question which has been traditionally posed in our community of churches over the centuries.

So, we have not scrupled to make minor, and a few major, emendations in order to include a lyric, despite the strictures of John Wesley. Such practice needs little justification if it is sensitively done. Asterisks will indicate where there are minor changes and any major alteration is duly acknowledged. Such emendations and alterations have been standard practice and, as Isaac Watts felt free to make David sing like a Christian, we can claim formidable precedents. Ultimately, we admitted no expression which was unscriptural.

As this is not an 'official' denominational book, we would be delighted if it were found useful across denominational frontiers. Of course, the tradition of our churches as evidenced in their inter-related history over three centuries is carefully nurtured in this book. But a tradition has to undergo some change and modification if it is to be a *living* tradition. Consequently, we have included a few lyrics which are implicitly or even explicitly trinitarian. We have chosen a few hymns which address Jesus Christ. These, we believe, are entirely consonant with our tradition. Those of us who, affirming the unipersonal God, nevertheless experience God as Father, as Son, as Holy Spirit, see no reason why we should not be able to sing that. Those of us who regard ourselves as disciples of the Lord Jesus Christ wish, from time to time, to address him in the manner that Stephen does in Acts ch.8 v.59. To those who may complain that such usage is *regressive*, we would suggest that a hymnal ought to try to bring forth from the store both things new *and* old. We live in an age when the richness and variety of biblical usage is more fully appreciated and the doctrinal rigidities of the past should not be allowed to inhibit us unduly. Besides, those who find such forms unacceptable, need not sing those hymns!

We have not attempted to impose any rigidly consistent principle in our revision or selection process. We see no reason why the traditional worship language of 'thee' and 'thou' should not co-exist with modern style. We have tried, within the limits already mentioned, to respect the integrity of each lyric. Indeed, we have restored the original wording where we thought it had been needlessly altered. We think that any major changes to our traditional language of worship would gravely injure our sense of belonging to the universal Church. We decided therefore to retain masculine forms of address and reference to God. We could not, however, defend language of worship which so often implies that our congregations have no women among them. Consequently, it has been a crucial and complex task to make the lyrics 'gender inclusive' wherever possible. Only in cases where there were copyright difficulties or where, on literary grounds, the changes seemed undesirable, have we failed to do this.

Good indexing of a hymn book incalculably increases its value and particularly to those who regularly conduct public worship. We are greatly indebted to Arthur Long for his careful work on the author index. We decided to leave some gaps where we could not be sure of details and would be grateful to have them plugged by helpful readers. Then, in a future reprint, we will be able to furnish a complete account. To have continued research would have further delayed the book.

The construction of the general thematic index has been for Tony Cross a long and arduous task. Pressures to abandon this project have been resisted. So, at last, we have an index which the leader of worship or devotional reader can use to locate all the major concepts relating to God, Jesus Christ, the Spirit of God, the Church, the Church's year, Christian worship, the Bible and Christian life. Well over 1,000 concepts are indexed and thousands of references. Such an index renders any cross-referencing in the body of the book superfluous. Large though the index is, we expect it to be straightforward to use once the sectional structure is grasped. Since so many of our acts of worship are organised *thematically*, such a compendium should swiftly indicate the relevant and key hymns. Leaders of worship sometimes claim that they have no need of such an aid: they know their customary hymn book inside out. But even *they* must have the occasional lapse of memory and, in this book, there are hymns new to our use.

We wish to record our grateful thanks for the timely support and encouragement of the Chalice Foundation and particularly for the management of the special Hymn Book account by the Foundation's treasurer, Mr Alan Coldwell. Without that support, the project might well have foundered at an earlier stage. We had generous donations without which we would not have been able to cope with our working expenses. But, above all, we are profoundly grateful to those congregations who sent in their paid orders in good time so that we were assured of the financial viability of the project. It is their subvention which has made the whole thing possible. They gave swiftly and more than doubled the value of their contribution. Moreover, they have been extraordinarily patient over the inevitable delay in publishing. We hope they feel that their wait has been rewarded by a book of real quality and usefulness.

It is perhaps not inappropriate to record our respective spheres of responsibility. Tony Cross had the dual role of business manager and literary editor. He liaised with the typesetters, designer and printers. Most taxing tasks of all: he made the lyrics gender inclusive wherever possible and compiled the thematic index. He is grateful to his long-suffering congregation at Mansford Street, Bethnal Green, for allowing him to devote so much time to the project. Arthur Long had the mammoth task of compiling the original sequence of hymns and, by use of a computer data-base, the indispensable listings and other indexes. Suggested tunes, too, for the most part were compiled by Arthur Long with some initial guidance from Andrew Grace, formerly organist at New Meeting Birmingham. Lena Baxter tackled the burdensome, complex and, at times, frustrating task of checking copyrights, negotiating permission to use and payment for use. Vernon Marshall was our convenor and host at New Meeting and, like all four of us, added his own valuable suggestions and judgements. The pleasantest feature of the whole enterprise has been our community of purpose and the way cheerfulness kept breaking through.

THE WORKING PARTY:

Lena Baxter, Tony Cross, Arthur Long, Vernon Marshall

Acknowledgements

WE GRATEFULLY acknowledge permission to use the following texts, on the understanding that this applies only to the first print run of *Hymns of Faith & Freedom*. Any future reproduction of these works should only be with the permission of the copyright holders listed in the middle column.

Author	*Permission granted by*	*Hymn*
ALINGTON, C. A.	Hymns Ancient & Modern Ltd	24
ARLOTT, John	The Author	459
BAX, Clifford	The Peters, Fraser & Dunlop Group	415
BAYLY, A. F.	Oxford University Press	231,400
BRIGGS, G. W.	Oxford University Press	76, 391
CARTER, Sydney	Stainer and Bell Ltd	130, 265, 319
CHISHOLM, Thomas O.	Hope Publishing Company, Carol Stream, IL 60188	54
CRUM, J. M. C.	Oxford University Press	168
DALE, Alan T.	Oxford University Press	262
DAVIES, Rupert E.	The Author	156
DEARMER, Geoffery	*Songs of Praise*: Oxford University Press	311
ELLIOT, John E.	The Author	133
FAHS, Sophia Lyon	The American Ethical Union	377
FARJEON, Eleanor	*The Children's Bells*: Oxford University Press	433
FOSDICK, H. E.	Mrs Elinor Downs	213
GALBRAITH, Peter	The Author	434
GREEN, F. Pratt	Stainer & Bell Ltd	53, 70, 351, 424
HARVEY, T. Edmund	Mr Richard S. Rowantree	345
HERFORD, Ruth	Miss Catherine Herford	398
HOLMES, John Haynes	Mr Roger W. Holmes	251, 303
HUGHES, Donald	Methodist Publishing House	471

ACKNOWLEDGEMENTS

Author	*Permission granted by*	*Hymn*
IKELER, Carol, Rose	*Songs and Hymns for Primary Children* © W.L. Jenkins: Westminster/John Knox Press	260
IVERSON, Daniel P.	The Moody Press	178
JONES, Richard	The Author	236
KAAN, Fred	Stainer & Bell Ltd	309
	Planting Trees and Sowing Seeds: Oxford University Press	408
KNIGHT, Sydney	The Author	366
LAFFERTY, Karen	Word Music UK, 9 Holdom Avenue, Bletchley, Milton Keynes MK1	272
MERRILL, W. P.	The Editor, *The Presbyterian Outlook*, Va. USA	228
MICKLEM, Caryl	The Author	286
OXENHAM, John	Mr Desmond Dunkerly	235
PERRY, Michael	Jubilate Hymns Ltd	105
PETTITT, Pamela	The Author	425
RADICE, William	The Author	461
REED, Clifford, M.	The Author	55, 166, 310, 462
SILLIMAN, Vincent	The American Ethical Union © 1955. Library Catalogue No. 54: 11625	422
SMITH, Jamie	The Author	104
SMITH, Leonard E. Jnr	Thankyou Music, PO Box 75, Eastbourne, East Sussex BN23 6NW	111
STONE, Lloyd C.	The Lorenz Corporation, PO Box 802, Dayton, Ohio OH 45401 0802	426
STRUTHER, Jan	*Enlarged Songs of Praise*: Oxford University Press	225, 256, 257
TWEEDY, Henry, Hallam	The Hymn Society, Texas Christian University, Fort Worth TX 76129	421
VALLANCE, Arthur	The Author's Executors	266
WREN, Brian A.	*Faith Looking Forward*: Oxford University Press	176

(We were advised that one hymn, "Sent forth by God's Blessing" by Omer Westendorf is in copyright to World Library Publishing Inc, Chicago, but, as our letter was returned marked "Unknown" we have assumed permission to print this hymn, with apologies for any infringement which may inadvertently have been caused).

We especially appreciate the opportunity to reproduce, free of charge, works by John E. Elliot, Sophia Lyon Fahs, Henry Emerson Fosdick, Peter Galbraith, T. Edmund Harvey, Ruth Herford, John Haynes Holmes, Daniel P. Iverson, Richard Jones, Sydney Knight, William Pierson Merrill, Caryl Micklem, Pamela Pettitt, William Radice, Clifford Reed, Vincent Silliman, Jamie Smith, and the late Arthur Vallance. We express special thanks to those authors and copyright holders who graciously allowed us to do so.

In spite of strenuous efforts to trace all copyright material, one or two items have so far proved totally elusive. However, most of these hymns appeared in *Hymns of Worship* (revised), on which this book is largely based. So we trust the authors would have no intrinsic objection to the use of their work again.

If we have offended in any way, we offer our sincere apologies and a promise to try to correct any mistakes or oversight when more information becomes available.

Finally, we acknowledge the generous help and advice we received in tracing copyright from the following:

Rev'd Sydney Knight (*Hymns for Living*)
Ms Joyce Horn (Oxford University Press)
Mr Derek Harris (Methodist Publishing House)
Ms Cecilia Tan (Beacon Press)
Ms Sylvia Carlisle (Friends' House)
Ms J. Wright (Canterbury Press, Norwich)

1

Old 100th L.M.

ALL people that on earth do dwell,
Sing to the Lord with cheerful voice;
Him serve with mirth, his praise forth tell;
Come ye before him and rejoice.

The Lord, ye know, is God indeed;
Without our aid he did us make;
We are his folk, he doth us feed;
And for his sheep he doth us take.

O enter, then, his gates with praise,
Approach with joy his courts unto;
Praise, laud, and bless his Name always,
For it is seemly so to do.

For why, the Lord our God is good,
His mercy is for ever sure;
His truth at all times firmly stood,
And shall from age to age endure.

W. Kethe

2

Ombersley L.M.

LORD of all being! throned afar,
Thy glory flames from sun and star;
Centre and soul of every sphere,
Yet to each loving heart how near!

Sun of our life! Thy quickening ray
Sheds on our path the glow of day;
Star of our hope! Thy softened light
Cheers the long watches of the night.

Our midnight is thy smile withdrawn;
Our noontide is thy gracious dawn;
Our rainbow arch thy mercy's sign;
All, save the clouds of sin, are thine.

Lord of all life, below, above,
Whose light is truth, whose warmth is love,
Before thy ever-blazing throne
We ask no lustre of our own.

Grant us thy truth to make us free,
And kindling hearts that burn for thee,
Till all thy living altars claim
One holy light, one heavenly flame.

O. W. Holmes

3

Melcombe L.M.

UNTO thy temple, Lord, we come
With thankful hearts to worship thee;
And pray that this may be our home
Until we touch eternity:

The common home of rich and poor,
Of bond and free, and great and small;
Large as thy love for evermore,
And warm and bright and good to all.

And dwell thou with us in this place,
Thou and thy Christ, to guide and bless;
Here make the well-springs of thy grace
Like fountains in the wilderness.

May thy whole truth be spoken here;
Thy gospel light for ever shine;
Thy perfect love cast out all fear,
And human life become divine.

R. Collyer

4

Luther's Hymn 87.87.887.

WE come unto our founders' God;
Their rock is our salvation;
The Eternal Arms, their dear abode,
We make our habitation.
We bring thee, Lord, the praise they brought,
We seek thee as thy saints have sought
In every generation.

Their joy unto their Lord we bring;
Their song to us descendeth;
The Spirit who in them did sing
To us his music lendeth.
His song in them, in us, is one;
We raise it high, we send it on:
The song that never endeth!

Ye saints to come, take up the strain:
The same sweet theme endeavour!
Unbroken be the Golden Chain!
Keep on the song for ever!
Safe in the same dear dwelling-place,
Rich in the same eternal grace,
Bless the same boundless Giver!

T. H. Gill

5

Wareham L.M.

O LORD! where'er thy people meet,
There they behold thy mercy-seat;
Where'er they seek thee, thou art found,
And every place is hallowed ground.

For thou, within no walls confined,
Inhabitest the humble mind;
Such ever bring thee where they come,
And going, take thee to their home.

Here may we prove the power of prayer
To strengthen faith, and lighten care;
To teach our faint desires to rise,
And bring all heaven before our eyes.

*William Cowper**

6

Darwall's 148th 66.66.44.44.

Ye holy angels bright,
Who wait at God's right hand,
Or through the realms of light
Fly at your Lord's command!
Assist our song,
Or else the theme
Too high doth seem
For mortal tongue.

Ye blessed souls at rest,
Who ran this earthly race,
And now, from sin released
Behold your Father's face!
His praises sound,
As in his light
With sweet delight
Ye do abound.

Ye saints, who toil below!
Adore your heavenly King,
And onward as ye go
Some joyful anthem sing;
Take what he gives;
And praise him still,
Through good and ill,
Who ever lives.

My soul, bear thou thy part;
Triumph in God above,
And with a well-tuned heart
Sing thou the songs of love!
  Let all thy days
  Till life shall end,
  Whate'er he send,
  Be filled with praise!

*Richard Baxter**

7

Lydia / Richmond C.M.

O FOR a thousand tongues to sing
  My Lord and Master's praise,
The glories of my God and King,
  The triumphs of his grace!

My gracious Master and my Lord,
  Assist me to proclaim,
To spread through all the earth abroad
  The honours of thy name.

Jesus – the name that charms our fears,
  That bids our sorrows cease;
'Tis music in the sinner's ears,
  'Tis life, and health, and peace.

He speaks; and, listening to his voice,
  New life the dead receive;
The mournful, broken hearts rejoice;
  The humble poor believe.

Hear him, ye deaf; his praise, ye dumb,
  Your loosened tongues employ;
Ye blind, behold your saviour come;
  And leap, ye lame, for joy!

In Christ, our Head, you then shall know,
  Shall feel, your sins forgiven,
Anticipate your heaven below,
  And own that love is heaven.

Charles Wesley (altered)

8

Repton *86.886.*

DEAR Lord and Father of mankind,
Forgive our foolish ways;
Reclothe us in our rightful mind;
In purer lives thy service find,
In deeper reverence, praise.

In simple trust like theirs who heard
Beside the Syrian sea
The gracious calling of the Lord,
Let us, like them, without a word
Rise up and follow thee.

O sabbath rest by Galilee!
O calm of hills above,
Where Jesus knelt to share with thee
The silence of eternity,
Interpreted by love!

With that deep hush subduing all
Our words and works that drown
The tender whisper of thy call,
As noiseless let thy blessing fall
As fell thy manna down.

Drop thy still dews of quietness,
Till all our strivings cease;
Take from our souls the strain and stress,
And let our ordered lives confess
The beauty of thy peace.

Breathe through the heats of our desire
Thy coolness and thy balm;
Let sense be dumb, let flesh retire;
Speak through the earthquake, wind and fire,
O still small voice of calm!

J. G. Whittier

9

Winchester New L.M.

O LIFE that makest all things new,
The world around, the mind within;
Our pilgrim feet, wet with thy dew,
In gladness hither turn again.

From hand to hand the greeting flows,
From eye to eye the signals run,
From heart to heart the bright hope glows;
The seekers of the light are one:

One in the freedom of the truth,
One in the joy of paths untrod,
One in the soul's perennial youth,
One in the larger thought of God;

The freer step, the fuller breath,
The wide horizon's grander view;
The sense of life that knows no death,
The life that maketh all things new.

*S. Longfellow**

10

Merton 87.87.

GOD is in his holy temple;
Earthly thoughts be silent now,
While with reverence we assemble
And before his presence bow.

He is with us now and ever
When we call upon his name,
Aiding every good endeavour,
Guiding every upward aim.

God is in his holy temple:
In the pure and holy mind,
In the reverent heart and simple,
In the soul from sense refined.

Then let every low emotion
  Banished far and silent be,
And our souls in pure devotion,
  Lord, be temples worthy of thee.

Hymns of the Spirit, 1864

11

St. Magnus C.M.

HOW lovely are thy dwellings, Lord,
  From noise and trouble free!
How beautiful the sweet accord
  Of souls that pray to thee!

Lord God of Hosts, that reign'st on high,
  They are the truly blest,
Who only will on thee rely,
  In thee alone will rest.

They pass refreshed the thirsty vale,
  The dry and barren ground,
As through a fruitful, watery dale,
  Where springs and showers abound.

They journey on from strength to strength,
  With joyful, hopeful cheer,
Till all before our God at length
  In Zion do appear.

For God the Lord, both sun and shield,
  Gives grace and glory bright:
No good from them shall be withheld
  Whose ways are just and right.

*John Milton and James Martineau**

12

Angelus L.M.

O GOD, whose presence glows in all
Within, around us, and above:
Thy word we bless, thy name we call,
Whose word is Truth whose name is Love.

That truth be with the heart believed
Of all who seek this sacred place,
With power proclaimed, in peace received:
Our spirit's light, thy Spirit's grace.

That love its holy influence pour,
To keep us kind and make us free,
And throw its binding blessing more
Round each with all, and all with thee.

Send down its angel to our side,
Send in its calm upon the breast;
For we would need no other guide,
And we can need no other rest.

*N. L. Frothingham**

13

Maryton L.M.

SPIRIT of grace, and health, and power,
Fountain of light and love below,
Abroad thy healing influence shower;
On all thy servants let it flow.

Inflame our hearts with perfect love;
In us the work of faith fulfil;
So not heaven's host shall swifter move
Than we on earth to do thy will.

Father! 'tis thine each day to yield
Thy children's wants a fresh supply;
Thou cloth'st the lilies of the field,
And hearest the young ravens cry.

On thee we cast our care; we live
Through thee, who know'st our every need;
O feed us with thy grace, and give
Our souls this day the living bread!

John Wesley

14

Cambridge S.M.

LORD, in this sacred hour,
Within thy courts we bend;
And bless thy love and own thy power,
Our father and our friend!

But thou art not alone
In courts by mortals trod;
Nor only is the day thine own
When we draw near to God.

Thy temple is the arch
Of yon unmeasured sky;
Thy sabbath, the stupendous march
Of grand eternity.

Lord, may that holier day
Dawn on thy servants' sight!
And grant us in those courts to pray
Of pure, unclouded light.

*S. G. Bulfinch**

15

Da Christus geboren war 77.77.

SOVEREIGN and transforming Grace,
We invoke thy quickening power;
Reign the spirit of this place,
Bless the purpose of this hour.

This thy house, the house of prayer;
This the day we hallow thine.
O let now thy grace appear,
Hallowing every place and time.

Holy and creative Light,
We invoke thy kindling ray;
Dawn upon our spirits' night,
Turn our darkness into day.

To the anxious soul impart
Hope, all other hopes above;
Stir the dull and hardened heart
With a longing and a love.

Work in all; in all renew
Day by day the life divine;
All our wills to thee subdue;
All our hearts to thee incline.

F. H. Hedge

16

Diva Servatrix / Integer Vitae 11 11 11.5.

FATHER, O hear us, seeking now to praise thee!
Thou art our hope, our confidence, our Saviour;
Thou art the refuge of the generations,
Lord God Almighty.

Maker of all things, loving all thy creatures,
God of all goodness, infinite in mercy,
Changeless, eternal, holiest and wisest,
Hear thou thy children.

We are thy children, asking thee to bless us,
Banded together for a full obedience,
Mutual help and mutual refreshing,
Lord, in thy service.

Childhood shall learn to know thee and revere thee;
Adulthood serve thee, strong in power and knowledge;
Old age shall trust thee, having felt thy mercy,
E'en 'mid the shadows.

Bless thou our purpose, consecrate our labours,
Keep us still faithful to the best and truest,
Guide us, protect us, make us not unworthy
Learners of Jesus.

Glory and honour, thanks and adoration,
Still will we bring, O God of earth and heaven,
To thee, the holy, merciful and mighty,
Father, our Father!

*D. Walmsley**

17

Stabat Mater 88.7.

GRACIOUS Power, the world pervading,
Blessing all, and none upbraiding,
We are met to worship thee.

By thy wisdom mind is lighted,
By thy love the heart excited,
Light and love all flow from thee;

And the soul of thought and feeling
In the voice thy praises pealing,
Must thy noblest homage be.

Not alone in our devotion;
In all being, life, and motion,
We the present Godhead see.

Gracious Power, the world pervading
Blessing all, and none upbraiding,
We are met to worship thee.

W. J. Fox

18

Was Lebet / Sanctissimus 12 10.12 10.

O WORSHIP the Lord in the beauty of holiness!
Bow down before him, his glory proclaim;
With gold of obedience and incense of lowliness,
Kneel and adore him, the Lord is his name.

Low at his feet lay thy burden of carefulness;
High on his heart he will bear it for thee,
Comfort thy sorrows, and answer thy prayerfulness,
Guiding thy steps as may best for thee be.

Fear not to enter his courts in the slenderness
Of the poor wealth thou wouldst reckon as thine;
Truth in its beauty, and love in its tenderness,
These are the offerings to lay on his shrine.

O worship the Lord in the beauty of holiness!
Bow down before him, his glory proclaim;
With gold of obedience and incense of lowliness,
Kneel and adore him, the Lord is his name.

J. S. B. Monsell

19

Nicaea *11 12.12 10.*

HOLY, holy, holy, Lord God Almighty!
Gratefully adoring our song shall rise to thee.
Holy, holy, holy, merciful and mighty,
Who wert, and art, and evermore shalt be.

Holy, holy, holy, though the darkness hide thee,
Though the eyes of sinful ones thy glory may not see;
Only thou art holy: there is none beside thee,
Perfect in power, in love, and purity.

Holy, holy, holy, Lord God Almighty!
All thy works shall praise thy name, in earth and sky
and sea.
Holy, holy, holy, merciful and mighty,
Who wert, and art, and evermore shalt be.

*R. Heber**

20

Stracathro *C.M.*

BEHOLD us, Lord, a little space
From daily tasks set free,
And met within thy holy place
To rest awhile with thee.

Around us rolls the ceaseless tide
Of business, toil and care,
And scarcely can we turn aside
For one brief hour of prayer.

Yet these are not the only walls
Wherein thou may'st be sought;
On homeliest work thy blessing falls,
In truth and patience wrought.

Thine are the loom, the forge, the mart,
The wealth of land and sea,
The worlds of science and of art
Revealed and ruled by thee.

Then let us prove our heavenly birth
In all we do and know;
And claim the kingdom of the earth
For thee, and not thy foe.

Work shall be prayer, if all be wrought
As thou wouldst have it done;
And prayer, by thee inspired and taught,
Itself with work be one.

J. Ellerton

21

Hanover 10 10.11 11.

O WORSHIP the King, all glorious above;
O gratefully sing his power and his love;
Our shield and defender, the Ancient of Days,
Pavilioned in splendour and girded with praise.

The earth with its store of wonders untold,
Almighty, thy power hath founded of old;
Hath stablished it fast by a changeless decree,
And round it hath cast like a mantle the sea.

Thy bountiful care what tongue can recite?
It breathes in the air, it shines in the light;
It streams from the hills, it descends to the plain,
And sweetly distils in the dew and the rain.

Frail children of dust, and feeble as frail,
In thee do we trust, nor find thee to fail;
Thy mercies how tender, how firm to the end,
Our Maker, Defender, Redeemer, and Friend!

O measureless Might! ineffable Love!
While angels delight to hymn thee above,
Thy humbler creation, though feeble their lays,
With true adoration shall sing to thy praise.

*Sir Robert Grant**

22

Lobe den Herren 14 14.4.7.8.

PRAISE to the Lord, the Almighty, the King of creation;
O my soul, praise him, for he is thy health and
salvation:
All ye who hear,
Now to his temple draw near,
Joining in glad adoration.

Praise to the Lord, who o'er all things so wondrously
reigneth,
Shelters thee under his wings, yea, so gently sustaineth:
Hast thou not seen
How thy entreaties have been
Granted in what he ordaineth?

Praise to the Lord, who doth prosper thy work and
defend thee;
Surely his goodness and mercy shall daily attend thee:
Ponder anew
What the Almighty can do,
Who with his love doth befriend thee.

Praise to the Lord! O let all that is in me adore him!
All that hath life and breath come now with praises
before him!
Let the Amen
Sound from his people again:
Gladly for aye we adore him!

J. Neander, trans. Catherine Winkworth and others

23

Monkland 77.77.

LET us with a gladsome mind
Praise the Lord, for he is kind:
For his mercies aye endure,
Ever faithful, ever sure.

Let us blaze his name abroad,
For of gods he is the God:

He, with all-commanding might,
Filled the new-made world with light:

He the golden-tressèd sun
Caused all day his course to run:

And the silver moon by night,
'Mid her spangled sisters bright:

He his chosen race did bless
In the barren wilderness:

All things living he doth feed,
His full hand supplies their need:

Let us then with gladsome mind
Praise the Lord, for he is kind:

*John Milton**

24

Corinth / Regent Square 87.87.87.

LORD of beauty, thine the splendour
Shewn in earth and sky and sea,
Burning sun and moonlight tender,
  Hill and river, flower and tree;
Lest we fail our praise to render
  Touch our eyes that they may see.

Lord of wisdom, whom obeying
  Mighty waters ebb and flow,
While unhasting, undelaying,
  Planets on their courses go;
In thy laws thyself displaying,
  Teach our minds thyself to know.

Lord of life, alone sustaining
  All below and all above,
Lord of love, by whose ordaining
  Sun and stars sublimely move;
In our earthly spirits reigning,
  Lift our hearts that we may love.

Lord of beauty, bid us own thee,
  Lord of truth, our footsteps guide,
Till as Love our hearts enthrone thee,
  And, with vision purified,
Lord of all, when all have known thee,
  Thou in all art glorified.

C. A. Alington

25

Leoni *66.84.D.*

PRAISE to the living God!
  All praisèd be his Name,
Who was, and is, and is to be,
  For aye the same!
The One Eternal God
  Ere aught that now appears:
The First, the Last, beyond all thought
  His timeless years!

Formless, all lovely forms
  Declare his loveliness;
Holy, no holiness of earth
  Can his express.
Lo, he is Lord of all!
  Creation speaks his praise,
And everywhere, above, below,
  His will obeys.

His Spirit floweth free,
  High surging where it will;
In prophet's word he spoke of old:
  He speaketh still.
Established is his law,
  And changeless it shall stand,
Deep writ upon the human heart,
  On sea, or land.

Eternal life hath he
  Implanted in the soul;
His love shall be our strength and stay
  While ages roll.
Praise to the living God!
  All praisèd be his Name
Who was, and is, and is to be,
  For aye the same!

Daniel Ben Judah

26

Laudes Domini 666.666.

WHEN morning gilds the skies
My heart awaking cries:
  "Thy name, O God, be praised."
Alike at work or prayer
To thee do I repair:
  "Thy name, O God, be praised."

Does sadness fill my mind?
A solace here I find,
  "Thy name, O God, be praised."
Or fades my earthly bliss?
My comfort still is this,
  "Thy name, O God, be praised."

When sleep her balm denies,
My silent spirit sighs,
  "Thy name, O God, be praised."
When evil thoughts molest,
With this I shield my breast,
  "Thy name, O God, be praised."

Be this, while life is mine,
My canticle divine,
  "Thy name, O God, be praised";
Be this the eternal song
Through all the ages long,
  "Thy name, O God, be praised."

*from the German, trans. E. Caswall**

27

Cwm Rhondda 87.87.47.

GOD is Love, by him upholden
Hang the glorious orbs of light,
In their language, glad and golden,
Speaking to us day and night
Their great story,
God is Love, and God is Might.

And the teeming earth rejoices
In that message from above,
With ten thousand thousand voices
Telling back, from hill and grove,
Her glad story,
God is Might, and God is Love.

With these anthems of creation,
Mingling in harmonious strife,
Christian songs of Christ's salvation,
To the world with blessing rife,
Tell their story,
God is Love, and God is Life.

Up to God let each affection
Daily rise, and round him move,
Our whole lives one resurrection
To the Life of life above;
Their glad story,
God is Life, and God is Love.

J. S. B. Monsell

28

Thanksgiving L. M.

BOTH heaven and earth do worship thee,
Thou Father of eternity!
With splendour from thy glory spread
Are heaven and earth replenishèd.

To thee all angels loudly cry,
The heavens and all the powers on high,
The apostles' glorious company,
The prophets' fellowship, praise thee.

The noble and victorious host
Of martyrs make of thee their boast;
The holy church, in every place,
Throughout the earth exalts thy praise.

From day to day, O Lord, do we
Highly exalt and honour thee;
Thy name we worship and adore,
World without end for evermore.

Vouchsafe, O Lord, we humbly pray,
To keep us safe from sin this day;
O Lord, have mercy on us all,
Have mercy on us when we call!

Latin Hymn

29

Praise, my soul 87.87.87

PRAISE, my soul, the King of Heaven,
  To his feet thy tribute bring;
Ransomed, healed, restored, forgiven,
  Evermore his praises sing:
Alleluia, Alleluia!
  Praise the everlasting King.

Praise him for his grace and favour
  To our forebears in distress;
Praise him still the same for ever,
  Slow to chide, and swift to bless;
Alleluia, Alleluia!
  Glorious in his faithfulness.

Father-like, he tends and spares us;
  Well our feeble frame he knows;
In his hands he gently bears us,
  Rescues us from all our foes;
Alleluia, Alleluia!
  Widely yet his mercy flows.

Angels in the height, adore him;
  Ye behold him face to face;
Saints triumphant, bow before him,
  Gathered in from every race;
Alleluia, Alleluia!
  Praise with us the God of grace.

*H. F. Lyte**

30

St. Denio 11 11.11 11.

IMMORTAL, invisible, God only wise,
In light inaccessible hid from our eyes,
Most blessèd, most glorious, the Ancient of Days,
Almighty, victorious, thy great Name we praise.

Unresting, unhasting, and silent as light,
Nor wanting, nor wasting, thou rulest in might;
Thy justice like mountains high soaring above
Thy clouds, which are fountains of goodness and love.

To all life thou givest, to both great and small;
In all life thou livest, the true life of all;
We blossom and flourish as leaves on the tree,
And wither and perish; but nought changeth thee.

Great Father of glory, pure Father of light,
Thine angels adore thee, all veiling their sight;
All laud we would render: O help us to see
'Tis only the splendour of light hideth thee.

W. C. Smith

31

Angel Voices 85.85.843.

ANGEL voices, ever singing
Round thy throne of light;
Angel harps for ever ringing,
  Rest not day nor night;
Thousands only live to bless thee
  And confess thee
  Lord of might.

Thou who art beyond the farthest
Mortal eye can see,
Can it be that thou regardest
Songs we raise to thee?
Yea, we know that thou art near us
And wilt hear us
Graciously.

Yea, we know that thou rejoicest
O'er each work of thine;
Thou didst ears and hands and voices
For thy praise design;
Craft and art and music's measure
For thy pleasure
All combine.

In thy house, great God, we offer
Of thine own to thee,
And for thine acceptance proffer,
All unworthily,
Hearts and minds and hands and voices
In our choicest
Psalmody.

Honour, glory, might and merit
Thine shall ever be,
God Eternal, Holy Spirit,
Boundless, pure and free;
Of the best that thou hast given
Earth and Heaven
Render thee.

*F. Pott**

32

Lasst uns erfreuen *L.M. with Alleluias*

WATCHERS unseen who nobly wrought,
Souls of the slain who bravely fought,
Raise the glad strain, Alleluia!
Makers of songs in ancient days,
Sing once again the hymn of praise, *Alleluia!*

Praise him, ye poor who knew no rest,
All who with hope were never blest,
  Bond and free folk, Alleluia!
Joy hath he brought to martyrs strong;
All saints triumphant raise the song, *Alleluia!*

Praise him on earth, all people then;
Praise him in worlds beyond our ken.
  God the Father, Alleluia!
All souls in far-off days to be,
Praise him to all eternity, *Alleluia!*

Fountain of faith and hope and love,
Lord of the starry skies above,
  Great Creator! Alleluia!
Light of all wisdom ever sought,
Higher than highest human thought! *Alleluia!*

*R. P. Howgrave-Graham**

33

Lasst uns erfreuen L.M. with Alleluias

ALL creatures of our God and King,
Lift up your voice and with us sing
  Alleluia, Alleluia!
Thou burning sun with golden beam,
Thou silver moon with softer gleam,
O praise him, O praise him, Alleluia, Alleluia, Alleluia!

Thou rushing wind that art so strong,
Ye clouds that sail in heaven along,
  O praise him, Alleluia!
Thou rising morn, in praise rejoice,
Ye lights of evening, find a voice.

Thou flowing water, pure and clear,
Make music for thy Lord to hear,
  Alleluia, Alleluia!
Thou fire so masterful and bright,
That givest us both warmth and light.

Dear mother earth, who day by day
Unfoldest blessings on our way,
O praise him, Alleluia!
The flowers and fruit that in thee grow,
Let them his glory also show.

And all ye folk of tender heart,
Forgiving others, take your part,
O sing ye, Alleluia!
Ye, who long pain and sorrow bear,
Praise God and on him cast your care.

And thou most kind and gentle death,
Waiting to hush our latest breath,
O praise him, Alleluia!
Thou leadest home the child of God,
And Christ our Lord the way hath trod.

Let all things their Creator bless,
And worship him in humbleness,
O praise him, Alleluia!
Praise, praise your Maker and your King,
Lift up your voice and with us sing.

*St. Francis of Assisi, trans. W. H. Draper**

34

Glasgow C.M.

SING forth his high eternal name
Who holds all powers in thrall,
Through endless ages still the same,
The mighty Lord of all.

His goodness, strong and measureless,
Upholds us lest we fall;
His hand is still outstretched to bless,
The loving Lord of all.

His perfect law defines and bounds:
Our strong defence and wall;
His providence our life surrounds,
The saving Lord of all.

He every thought and every deed
  Doth to his judgment call;
Oh, may our hearts obedient heed
  The righteous Lord of all.

When, turning from forbidden ways,
  Low at his feet we fall,
His strong and tender arms upraise,
  The pardoning Lord of all.

Unwearied he is working still,
  Unspent his blessings fall,
Almighty, loving, righteous One,
  The only Lord of all.

*S. Longfellow**

35

Blaenwern / Laus Deo 87.87.D. or 87.87.

BRIGHT the vision that delighted
  Once the sight of Judah's seer;
Sweet the countless tongues united
  To entrance the prophet's ear.

Round the Lord in glory seated
  Cherubim and seraphim
Filled his temple, and repeated
  Each to each the alternate hymn:

"Lord thy glory fills the heaven;
  Earth is with its fulness stored;
Unto thee be glory given,
  Holy, holy, holy Lord!"

Heaven is still with glory ringing,
  Earth takes up the angels' cry,
"Holy, holy, holy," singing,
  "Lord of hosts, the Lord most high."

With his seraph host before him,
  With his holy church below,
Thus unite we to adore him,
  Bid we thus our anthem flow:

"Lord, thy glory fills the heaven;
Earth is with its fulness stored;
Unto thee be glory given,
Holy, holy, holy Lord!"

R. Mant

36

Luckington 10 4.66.66.10 4.

LET all the world in every corner sing
"My God and King!"
The heavens are not too high,
His praise may thither fly:
The earth is not too low;
His praises there may grow.
Let all the world in every corner sing
"My God and King!"

Let all the world in every corner sing
"My God and King!"
The Church with psalms must shout,
No door can keep them out:
But, above all, the heart
Must bear the longest part.
Let all the world in every corner sing
"My God and King!"

George Herbert

37

Martins 10 10.7.

SING Alleluia forth in ardent praise,
O citizens of heaven, and gladly raise
An endless Alleluia.

Ye Powers who stand before the Eternal Light,
In hymning choirs re-echo to the height
An endless Alleluia.

Ye who have gained at length your palms in bliss,
Victorious ones, your chant shall still be this –
An endless Alleluia.

The Holy City shall take up your strain,
And with glad songs resounding wake again
An endless Alleluia.

In blissful antiphons ye thus rejoice
To render to the Lord with thankful voice
An endless Alleluia.

There, in one grand acclaim, for ever ring
The strains which tell the honour of your King,
An endless Alleluia.

While thee, Creator of the world, we praise
For ever, and tell out through all our days
An endless Alleluia.

To thee, Eternal God, our voices sing
Glory for evermore; to thee we bring
An endless Alleluia.

Mozarabic, trans. J. Ellerton and others

38

Austria 87.87.D.

PRAISE the Lord! ye heavens adore him,
Praise him, angels in the height,
Sun and moon, rejoice before him,
Praise him, all ye stars of light!
Praise the Lord, for he hath spoken;
Worlds his mighty voice obeyed;
Laws which never shall be broken
For their guidance he hath made.

Praise the Lord, for he is glorious;
Never shall his promise fail;
God hath made his saints victorious;
Sin and death shall not prevail.
Praise the God of our salvation;
Hosts on high, his power proclaim!
Heaven and earth and all creation
Praise and magnify his name!

Foundling Hospital Collection, 1796

39

Simeon *L.M.*

PRAISE ye the Lord, 'tis good to raise
Our hearts and voices in his praise:
His nature and his works invite
To make this duty our delight.

He formed the stars, those heavenly flames,
He counts their numbers, calls their names;
His wisdom's vast, and knows no bound,
A deep where all our thoughts are drowned.

Sing to the Lord, exalt him high,
Who spreads his clouds along the sky;
There he prepares the fruitful rain,
Nor lets the drops descend in vain.

He makes the grass the hills adorn,
And clothes the smiling fields with corn;
The beasts with food his hands supply,
And the young ravens when they cry.

His saints are lovely in his sight,
He views his children with delight;
He sees their hope, he knows their fear,
And looks, and loves his image there.

Isaac Watts

40

Heathlands *77.77.77.*

O GIVE thanks to him who made
Morning light and evening shade;
Source and giver of all good,
Nightly sleep and daily food;
Quickener of our wearied powers,
Guard of our unconscious hours.

O give thanks to Nature's King,
Who made every breathing thing:
His our warm and sentient frame,
His the mind's immortal flame;
Oh, how close the ties that bind
Spirits to the eternal Mind!

O give thanks with heart and lip,
For we are his workmanship,
And all creatures are his care:
Not a bird that cleaves the air
Falls unnoticed; so let all
God's great love to us recall.

*J. Conder**

41

England's Lane 77.77.77.

FOR the beauty of the earth,
For the splendour of the skies,
For the love which from our birth
Over and around us lies:
Father, unto thee we raise
This, our sacrifice of praise.

For the wonder of each hour
Of the day and of the night,
Hill and vale, and tree and flower,
Sun and moon, and stars of light:

For the joy of ear and eye,
For the heart and mind's delight,
For the mystic harmony
Linking sense to sound and sight:

For the joy of human love,
Brother, sister, parent, child,
Friends on earth, and friends above,
For all gentle thoughts and mild:

For thy Church that evermore
Lifteth holy hands above,
Offering up on every shore
Its pure sacrifice of love:

*F. S. Pierpoint**

42

Ratisbon 77.77.77.

GOD of mercy, God of grace,
Show the brightness of thy face;
Shine upon us, Father, shine,
Fill us with thy light divine;
And thy saving health extend
Unto earth's remotest end.

Let the people praise thee, Lord!
Let thy love on all be poured;
Let awakened nations sing
Glory to their heavenly King,
At thy feet their tribute pay,
And thy holy will obey.

Let the people praise thee, Lord!
Earth shall then her fruits afford,
God to us his blessing give,
We to God devoted live;
All below, and all above,
One in joy and light and love.

*H. F. Lyte**

43

Gwalchmai 74.74.D

KING of glory, King of peace,
  I will love thee;
And that love may never cease,
  I will move thee.
Thou hast granted my request,
  Thou hast heard me;
Thou didst note my working breast,
  Thou hast spared me.

Wherefore with my utmost art
I will sing thee,
And the cream of all my heart
I will bring thee.
Though my sins against me cried,
Thou didst clear me;
And alone, when they replied,
Thou didst hear me.

Seven whole days, not one in seven,
I will praise thee;
In my heart, though not in heaven,
I can raise thee.
Small it is, in this poor sort
To enrol thee:
E'en eternity's too short
To extol thee.

George Herbert

44

Contemplation C.M.

WHEN all thy mercies, O my God,
My rising soul surveys,
Transported with the view, I'm lost
In wonder, love, and praise.

Unnumbered comforts on my soul
Thy tender care bestowed,
Before my infant heart conceived
From whom those comforts flowed.

Ten thousand thousand precious gifts
My daily thanks employ,
Nor is the least a cheerful heart
That tastes those gifts with joy.

Through every period of my life
Thy goodness I'll pursue,
And after death, in distant worlds,
The glorious theme renew.

Through all eternity to thee
  A joyful song I'll raise;
For O eternity's too short
  To utter all thy praise!

Joseph Addison

45

Almsgiving 888.4.

O LORD of heaven, and earth, and sea,
To thee all praise and glory be;
How shall we show our love to thee,
  Who givest all?

The golden sunshine, vernal air,
Fair flowers and fruit, thy love declare;
When harvests ripen, thou art there,
  Who givest all.

For peaceful homes, and healthful days,
For all the blessings earth displays,
We owe thee thankfulness and praise,
  Who givest all.

For souls redeemed, for sins forgiven,
For means of grace and hopes of heaven,
Father, what can to thee be given,
  Who givest all?

We lose what on ourselves we spend,
We have as treasure without end
Whatever, Lord, to thee we lend,
  Who givest all:

To thee, from whom we all derive
Our life, our gifts, our power to give;
Oh, may we ever with thee live,
  Who givest all!

*C. Wordsworth**

46

Crüger 76.76. D.

WITH happy voices ringing,
Thy children, Lord, appear,
Their joyous praises bringing
In anthems sweet and clear;
For skies of golden splendour,
For azure rolling sea,
For blossoms fair and tender,
O Lord, we worship thee.

What though no eye beholds thee,
No hand thy hand may feel,
Thy universe unfolds thee,
Thy starry heavens reveal;
The earth and all its glory,
Our homes and all we love,
Tell forth the wondrous story
Of One who reigns above.

And shall we not adore thee
With more than joyous song,
And live in truth before thee
All beautiful and strong?
Lord, bless our souls' endeavour
Thy servants true to be,
And through all life, for ever,
To live our praise to thee.

*W. G. Tarrant**

47

Beethoven 87.87. D.

JOYFUL, joyful, we adore thee,
God of glory, Lord of love;
Hearts unfold like flowers before thee,
Hail thee as the sun above!
Melt the clouds of sin and sadness;
Drive the dark of doubt away;
Giver of immortal gladness,
Fill us with the light of day.

All thy works with joy surround thee,
  Earth and heaven reflect thy rays,
Stars and angels sing around thee,
  Centre of unbroken praise;
Field and forest, vale and mountain,
  Flowering meadow, flashing sea,
Chanting bird and flowing fountain
  Call us to rejoice in thee.

Thou art giving and forgiving,
  Ever blessing, ever blest,
Well-spring of the joy of living,
  Ocean-depth of happy rest!
Thou the Father, Christ our Brother,
  All who live in love are thine;
Teach us how to love each other,
  Lift us to the joy divine.

Mortals join the mighty chorus,
  Which the morning stars recall;
Father-love is reigning o'er us,
  Kindred love binds each to all;
Ever singing march we onward,
  Victors in the midst of strife;
Joyful music lifts us sunward
  In the triumph song of life.

*H. van Dyke**

48

Wiltshire C.M.

THROUGH all the changing scenes of life,
  In trouble and in joy,
The praises of my God shall still
  My heart and tongue employ.

O magnify the Lord with me;
  With me exalt his name;
When in distress to him I called,
  He to my rescue came.

The hosts of God encamp around
The dwellings of the just;
Deliverance he affords to all
Who on his succour trust.

O make but trial of his love;
Experience will decide
How blest are they, and only they,
Who in his truth confide!

Fear him, ye saints, and you will then
Have nothing else to fear;
Make you his service your delight,
Your wants shall be his care.

N. Tate and N. Brady

49

Gott will's machen 87.87.

LORD, we thank thee for the pleasure
That our happy lifetime gives,
The inestimable treasure
Of a soul that ever lives:

Mind that looks before and after,
Yearning for its home above;
Human tears and human laughter,
And the depth of human love;

For the thrill, the leap, the gladness
Of our pulses flowing free;
E'en for every touch of sadness
That may bring us nearer thee.

Teach us so our days to number
That we may be lowly-wise;
Dreary mist or cloud of slumber
Never dull our heavenward eyes.

Hearty be our work and willing,
As to thee not humankind;
For we know our souls' fulfilling
Is in heav'n – not here confined.

*T. W. Jex-Blake**

50

Wentworth 84.84.84.

MY God, I thank thee, who hast made
  The earth so bright,
So full of splendour and of joy,
  Beauty and light;
So many glorious things are here,
  Noble and right!

I thank thee, too, that thou hast made
  Joy to abound;
So many gentle thoughts and deeds
  Circling us round,
That in the darkest spot on earth
  Some love is found.

I thank thee more, that all our joy
  Is touched with pain;
That shadows fall on brightest hours;
  That thorns remain;
So that earth's bliss may be our guide,
  And not our chain.

For thou who knowest, Lord, how soon
  Our weak heart clings,
Hast given us joys tender and true,
  Yet all with wings;
So that we see, gleaming on high,
  Diviner things.

I thank thee, Lord, that thou hast kept
  The best in store:
We have enough, yet not too much
  To long for more,
A yearning for a deeper peace
  Not known before.

Adelaide A. Procter

51

Bow Brickhill *L.M.*

O THOU whose perfect goodness crowns
With peace and joy this sacred day,
Our hearts are glad for all the years
Thy love has kept us in thy way.

For common tasks of help and cheer,
For quiet hours of thought and prayer,
For moments when we seemed to feel
The breath of a diviner air;

For mutual love and trust that keep
Unchanged through all the changing time;
For friends within the veil who thrill
Our spirits with a hope sublime;

For truth that evermore makes free
From bonds of sect and bonds of creed;
For light that shines that we may see
Our own in every neighbour's need;

For this and more than words can say,
We praise and bless thy holy Name.
Come life or death: enough to know
That thou art evermore the same.

*J. W. Chadwick**

52

Kent *L.M.*

THOU One in all, thou All in one,
Source of the grace that crowns our days,
For all thy gifts 'neath cloud or sun,
We lift to thee our grateful praise.

We bless thee for the life that flows,
A pulse in every grain of sand,
A beauty in the blushing rose,
A thought and deed in brain and hand.

For life that thou hast made a joy,
For strength to make our lives like thine,
For duties that our hands employ,
We bring our offerings to thy shrine.

Be thine to give and ours to own
The truth that sets thy children free,
The law that binds us to thy throne,
The love that makes us one with thee.

S. C. Beach

53

Engelberg 10 10 10.4.

WHEN, in our music, God is glorified,
And adoration leaves no room for pride,
It is as though the whole creation cried:
Alleluia!

How often, making music, we have found
A new dimension in the world of sound,
As worship moved us to a more profound
Alleluia!

So has the Church, in liturgy and song,
In faith and love, through centuries of wrong,
Borne witness to the truth in every tongue:
Alleluia!

And did not Jesus sing a psalm that night
When utmost evil strove against the Light?
Then let us sing, for whom he won the fight:
Alleluia!

Let every instrument be tuned for praise!
Let all rejoice who have a voice to raise!
And may God give us faith to sing always:
Alleluia! Amen.

F. Pratt Green

54

Great is thy Faithfulness 11 10.11 10.

GREAT is thy faithfulness, O God my Father,
There is no shadow of turning with thee;
Thou changest not, thy compassions, they fail not;
As thou hast been thou for ever wilt be:

Great is thy faithfulness! Great is thy faithfulness!
Morning by morning new mercies I see;
All I have needed thy hand has provided.
Great is thy faithfulness, Lord, unto me.

Summer and winter, and springtime and harvest,
Sun, moon and stars in their courses above,
Join with all nature in manifold witness
To thy great faithfulness, mercy and love:

Pardon for sin and a peace that endureth,
Thy own dear presence to cheer and to guide;
Strength for today and bright hope for tomorrow,
Blessings all mine, with ten thousand beside!

Thomas O. Chisholm

55

Londonderry Air 11 10. 11 10. D

WISDOM divine, bright-shining never-fading,
Who soon is found by those who seek in love,
She waits outside our door for us to meet her,
To grant us peace all other things above.
She is our treasure, rich with wealth unmeasured,
From her pour forth the gifts that come to save,
Her teaching frees the soul entrapped and fettered,
To heed her is to be no more a slave.

She has a spirit, free and clear and holy,
All things she fills, with purity pervades
The whole creation, loving all its goodness;
From God she rises – nothing her degrades.
She is but one, all-potent and unchanging,
All things renews, all saintly souls indwells,
Her radiance outshines the brightest sunlight,
The world she spans, its darkness she dispels.

O beauteous Wisdom flowing from that mystery
Which we, in wondering awe, have named divine,
You are the guiding heart of the Creator,
And order all things with a will benign.
Come to me now and I, with love, will greet you,
Open my heart to all you have to teach,
I would know truth and self-control and justice,
And be your channel in my deeds and speech.

Clifford Martin Reed

56 *Love Divine/Blaenwern* 87.87. or 87.87.D.

LOVE divine, all loves excelling,
Joy of heaven, to earth come down,
Fix us in thy humble dwelling,
All thy faithful mercies crown.

Thou, O God, art all compassion,
Pure unbounded love thou art;
Visit us with thy salvation,
Enter every trembling heart.

Come, Almighty, to deliver,
Let us all thy grace receive;
Suddenly return and never,
Never more thy temples leave.

Thee we would be always blessing,
Serve thee as thy hosts above,
Pray, and praise thee, without ceasing,
Glory in thy perfect love.

Finish then thy new creation,
  Pure and spotless let us be;
Let us see thy great salvation,
  Perfectly restored in thee:

Changed from glory into glory,
  Till in heaven we take our place,
Till we cast our crowns before thee,
  Lost in wonder, love, and praise.

*Charles Wesley**

57

Abridge C.M.

O FOR a heart to praise my God,
  A heart from sin set free,
A heart that loves to run the road
  Thou openest, Lord, for me!

A heart resigned, submissive, meek,
  A fitting throne for thee,
Where Jesus' voice is heard to speak
  Of all thy love to me:

A humble, lowly, contrite heart,
  Believing, true, and clean;
Which neither life nor death can part
  From him that dwells within;

A heart in every thought renewed
  And full of love divine;
Perfect, and right, and pure, and good:
  A copy, Lord, of thine!

Thy nature, gracious Lord, impart;
  Come quickly from above;
Write thy new name upon my heart,
  Thy new, best name of Love.

*Charles Wesley**

58

St.Gall 87.87. D.(iambic)

A JOYFUL hymn of praise we sing,
  And thankfully we gather,
To bless the love of God above,
  Our everlasting Father.
    In him rejoice with heart and voice,
      Whose glory fadeth never,
    Whose providence is our defence,
      Who lives and loves for ever!

From shades of night he calls the light,
  And from the soil the flower;
From every cloud his blessings break,
  In sunshine or in shower.

Full in his sight his children stand,
  By his strong arm defended;
And he, whose wisdom guides the world,
  Our footsteps hath attended.

For nothing falls unknown to him –
  Or care, or joy, or sorrow –
And he whose mercy ruled the past
  Will be our stay tomorrow.

*A. N. Blatchford**

59

Harts 77.77.

EVER more as years roll round
Do thy mercies, Lord, abound;
Gifts untold on us descend
From the Love that hath no end.

Day by day thy doors of gold
Are for our delight unrolled;
Night by night thy shadows deep
Veil our eyes in kindly sleep.

Countless homes, with love made dear,
Feel thy sacred presence near;
Earth, with countless blossoms crowned,
Wafts her incense all around.

Ever more our hearts would give
Thanks to thee in whom we live,
And a grateful music bear
Through each hour of work or prayer.

*R. Wilton**

60

Chorus Angelorum C.M.

FILL thou my life, O Lord my God,
In every part with praise,
That my whole being may proclaim
Thy being and thy ways.

Not for the lip of praise alone,
Nor e'en the praising heart,
I ask, but for a life made up
Of praise in every part.

Praise in the common words I speak,
Life's common looks and tones;
In kindly talk at hearth and board
With my belovèd ones.

Praise in the common things of life,
Its goings out and in;
Praise in each duty and each deed,
However small and mean;

Not in the temple crowd alone
Where holy voices chime;
But in the silent paths of earth,
The quiet rooms of time.

So shall no part of day or night
From sacredness be free:
But all my life in every step,
Be fellowship with thee.

*H. Bonar**

61

Nun Danket 67.67.66.66.

NOW thank we all our God,
With heart, and hands, and voices,
Who wondrous things hath done,
In whom his world rejoices;
Who from our mother's arms
Hath blessed us on our way
With countless gifts of love,
And still is ours to-day.

Oh, may this bounteous God
Through all our life be near us,
With ever joyful hearts
And blessed peace to cheer us;
And keep us in his grace,
And guide us when perplexed,
And free us from all ills
In this world and the next.

All praise and thanks to God
The Father now be given;
We lift our hearts to him
Who reigns in highest heaven:
The One Eternal God,
Whom earth and heaven adore,
Who was of old, is now,
And shall be evermore.

*M. Rinckart, trans. Catherine Winkworth**

62

Gopsal 66.66.88.

REJOICE! the Lord is King:
Your Lord and King adore;
Mortals, give thanks and sing,
And triumph evermore:
Lift up your hearts, lift up your voice;
Rejoice again, I say rejoice!

His wintry north winds blow,
Loud tempests rush amain;
Yet his thick showers of snow
Defend the infant grain:

He wakes the genial spring,
Perfumes the balmy air;
The vales their tribute bring,
The promise of the year:

He leads the circling year;
His flocks the hills adorn;
He fills the golden ear,
And loads the field with corn:

Lead on your fleeting train,
Ye years, and months, and days;
O bring the eternal reign
Of love, and joy, and praise:

J. Taylor (v.i. Charles Wesley)

63

Firmament L.M.D.

THE spacious firmament on high,
With all the blue ethereal sky,
And spangled heavens, a shining frame,
Their great Original proclaim.
The unwearied sun, from day to day,
Doth his Creator's power display;
And publishes to every land
The work of an almighty hand.

Soon as the evening shades prevail,
The moon takes up the wondrous tale,
And nightly to the listening earth
Repeats the story of her birth;
Whilst all the stars that round her burn,
And all the planets in their turn,
Confirm the tidings as they roll,
And spread the truth from pole to pole.

What though in solemn silence all
Move round the dark terrestrial ball;
What though nor real voice nor sound
Amidst their radiant orbs be found;
In reason's ear they all rejoice,
And utter forth a glorious voice,
For ever singing as they shine,
"The hand that made us is divine."

Joseph Addison

64

St. Flavian *C.M.*

THERE is a book, who runs may read,
Which heavenly truth imparts,
And all the lore its scholars need,
Pure eyes and Christian hearts.

The works of God above, below,
Within us and around,
Are pages in that book, to show
How God himself is found.

The glorious sky embracing all
Is like the Maker's love,
Wherewith encompassed, great and small
In peace and order move.

The dew of heaven is like thy grace,
It steals in silence down;
But where it lights, the favoured place
By richest fruits is known.

Two worlds are ours: 'tis only sin
Forbids us to descry
The mystic heaven and earth within,
Plain as the sea and sky.

Thou who hast given me eyes to see
And love this sight so fair,
Give me a heart to find out thee,
And read thee everywhere.

J. Keble

65

Duke Street L.M.

GOD of the earth, the sky, the sea,
Maker of all above, below,
Creation lives and moves in thee,
Thy present life through all doth flow.

Thy love is in the sunshine's glow,
Thy life is in the quickening air;
When lightnings flash and storm-winds blow,
There is thy power; thy law is there.

We feel thy calm at evening's hour,
Thy grandeur in the march of night;
And, when the morning breaks in power,
We hear thy word, "Let there be light."

But higher far, and far more clear,
Thee in our spirit we behold:
Thine image and thyself are there,
The indwelling God, proclaimed of old.

*S. Longfellow**

66

Childhood 888.6.

GOD speaks to us in bird and song,
In winds that drift the clouds along,
Above the din of toil and wrong
A melody of love.

God speaks to us in far and near,
In peace of home and friends most dear,
From the dim past and present clear,
  A melody of love.

God speaks to us in darkest night,
By quiet ways through mornings bright,
When shadows fall with evening light,
  A melody of love.

God speaks to us in every land,
On wave-lapped shore and silent strand,
By kiss of child and touch of hand,
  A melody of love.

O Voice divine, speak thou to me,
Beyond the earth, beyond the sea;
First let me hear, then sing to thee
  A melody of love.

J. Johnson

67

St. Agnes 10 10.10 10.

SEEK not afar for beauty; lo! it glows
  In dew-wet grasses all about thy feet;
  In birds, in sunshine, in the smiles we meet,
In stars and mountain summits topped with snows.

Go not abroad for happiness: for see –
  It is a flower blooming at thy door.
  Bring love and justice home, and then no more
Thou'lt wonder in what dwelling joy may be.

Dream not of noble service elsewhere wrought;
  The simple duty that awaits thy hand
  Is God's voice speaking his divine command:
Life's common deeds build all that saints have thought.

In wonder-workings, or some bush aflame,
  We look for God and fancy him concealed;
  But in earth's common things he stands revealed,
While grass and flowers and stars spell out his name.

*M. J. Savage**

68

Gonfalon Royal L.M.

MYSTERIOUS Presence, Source of all,
The world without, the world within,
Fountain of life, O hear our call,
And pour thy living waters in.

Thou breathest in the rushing wind,
Thy Spirit stirs in leaf and flower;
Nor wilt thou from the willing mind
Withhold thy light and love and power.

Thy hand unseen to accents clear
Awoke the psalmist's trembling lyre,
And touched the lips of holy seer
With flame from thine own altar fire.

That touch divine still, Lord, impart,
Still give the prophet's burning word;
And vocal in each waiting heart
Let living psalms of praise be heard.

S. C. Beach

69

Galliard 77.77.

ALL that's good, and great, and true,
All that is, and is to be,
Be it old, or be it new,
Comes, O Father, comes from thee.

Mercies dawn with every day,
Newer, brighter than before;
And the sun's declining ray
Layeth others up in store.

Not a bird that doth not sing
Sweetest praises to thy name;
Not an insect on the wing
But thy wonders doth proclaim.

Every blade and every tree,
All in happy concert ring,
And in wondrous harmony
Join in praises to their King.

Far and near, o'er land and sea,
Mountain top and wooded dell,
All, in singing, sing to thee
Songs of love ineffable.

Fill us then with love divine;
Grant that we, though toiling here,
May, in spirit being thine,
See and hear thee everywhere.

G. Thring

70

Stewardship 11 10. 11 10.

GOD in his love for us lent us this planet,
Gave it a purpose in time and in space:
Small as a spark from the fire of creation,
Cradle of life and the home of our race.

Thanks be to God for its bounty and beauty,
Life that sustains us in body and mind:
Plenty for all, if we learn how to share it,
Riches undreamed-of to fathom and find.

Long have our human wars ruined its harvest;
Long has earth bowed to the terror of force;
Long have we wasted what others have need of,
Poisoned the fountain of life at its source.

Earth is the Lord's: it is ours to enjoy it,
Ours, as his stewards, to farm and defend.
From its pollution, misuse, and destruction,
Good Lord, deliver us, world without end!

F. Pratt Green

71

Nun Danket 67.67.66.66.

"WHERE is your God?" they say:
Answer them, Lord most holy!
Reveal thy secret way
Of visiting the lowly:
Not wrapped in moving cloud,
Or nightly-resting fire;
But veiled within the shroud
Of silent high desire.

Come not in flashing storm,
Or bursting frown of thunder;
Come in the viewless form
Of wakening love and wonder;
Of duty grown divine,
The restless spirit, still;
Of sorrows taught to shine,
As shadows of thy will.

O God! the pure alone –
E'en in their deep confessing –
Can see thee as their own,
And find the perfect blessing;
Yet to each waiting soul
Speak in thy still small voice,
Till broken love's made whole,
And saddened hearts rejoice.

James Martineau

72

St. Bernard C.M.

WE pray no more, made lowly wise,
For miracle and sign;
Anoint our eyes to see, within
The common, the divine.

"Lo here, lo there," no more we cry,
Dividing with our call
The mantle of thy presence, Lord,
That seamless covers all.

We turn from seeking thee afar
  And in unwonted ways,
To build from out our daily lives
  The temples of thy praise.

And if thy casual comings, Lord,
  To hearts of old were dear,
What joy shall dwell within the faith
  That feels thee ever near!

And nobler yet shall duty grow,
  And more shall worship be,
When thou art found in all our life,
  And all our life in thee.

F. L. Hosmer

73

Gerontius C.M.

GO not, my soul, in search of him,
  Thou wilt not find him there,
Or in the depths of shadow dim,
  Or heights of upper air.

For not in far-off realms of space
  The Spirit hath its throne;
In every heart it findeth place
  And waiteth to be known.

Thought answereth alone to thought,
  And soul with soul hath kin;
The outward God he findeth not
  Who finds not God within.

And if the vision come to thee
  Revealed by inward sign,
Earth will be full of Deity,
  And with his glory shine.

Thou shalt not want for company,
  Nor pitch thy tent alone;
The indwelling God will go with thee
  And show thee of his own.

Oh, gift of gifts, oh, grace of grace,
That God should condescend
To make thy heart his dwelling-place
And be thy daily Friend!

Then go not thou in search of him,
But to thyself repair;
Wait thou within the silence dim,
And thou shalt find him there.

F. L. Hosmer

74

Bow Brickhill L.M.

O LOVE of God, how strong and true!
Eternal and yet ever new;
Uncomprehended and unbought,
Beyond all knowledge and all thought.

O Love of God, how deep and great!
Far deeper than our deepest hate;
Self-fed, self-kindled like the light,
Eternal, changeless, infinite.

O heavenly Love, how precious still,
In days of weariness and ill,
In nights of pain and helplessness,
To heal, to comfort, and to bless!

O Love of God, our shield and stay
Through all the perils of our way!
Eternal Love, in thee we rest,
For ever safe, for ever blest.

*H. Bonar**

75

Drake's Boughton 87.87.

LONG ago the lilies faded
Which to Jesus seemed so fair,
But the love that bade them blossom
Still is working everywhere.

On the moors and in the valleys,
By the streams we love so well,
There is greater glory blooming
Than the human tongue can tell.

Long ago in sacred silence
Died the accents of his prayer;
Still the souls that seek the Father
Find his presence everywhere.

In the multitude adoring,
In the chamber sad and lone,
He is there to help and comfort,
As they pray, "Thy will be done!"

Let us seek him, still believing
He that worketh round us yet,
Clothing lilies in the meadows,
Will his children ne'er forget.

*W. G. Tarrant**

76

St. Matthias *88.88.88.*

LORD of all majesty and might,
Whose presence fills the unfathomed deep,
Wherein uncounted worlds of light
Through countless ages vigil keep;
Eternal God, can such as we,
Frail humankind, know aught of thee?

Beyond all knowledge thou art wise,
With wisdom that transcends all thought;
Yet still we seek with straining eyes,
Yea, seek thee as our forebears sought;
Nor will we from the quest depart
Till we shall know thee as thou art.

Frail though our form, and brief our day,
Our mind has bridged the gulf of years;
Our puny balances can weigh
The magnitude of starry spheres;
Within us is eternity;
Whence comes it, Father, but from thee?

For when thy wondrous works we view,
And mind gives answer back to mind,
Thine image stands revealed anew;
And, seeking, we shall surely find.
Thy people's heritage we claim;
Shall not thy children know thy name?

We know in part; enough we know
To walk with thee, and walk aright;
And thou shalt guide us as we go,
And lead us into fuller light,
Till, when we stand before thy throne,
We know at last as we are known.

*G. W. Briggs**

77

Truro L.M.

O FOR that flame of living fire
Which shone so bright in saints of old;
Which bade their souls to heaven aspire,
Calm in distress, in danger bold.

O for the spirit which of old
Proclaimed thy love and taught thy ways,
Forth in Isaiah's thunder rolled,
Breathed in the psalmist's tenderest lays.

O for that spirit, Lord, which dwelt
In Jesus' breast and sealed him thine;
Which made Paul's heart with sorrow melt,
And glow with energy divine.

Is not thy word as mighty now
As when the prophets felt its power?
The ancient days remember thou,
The ancient inspiration shower.

Anon.

78

Kilmarnock C.M.

ONE thought I have, my ample creed,
  So deep it is and broad,
And equal to my every need –
  It is the thought of God.

Each morn unfolds some fresh surprise
  In paths till now untrod;
And rising in my inner skies
  Shines forth the thought of God.

At night my gladness is my prayer;
  I drop my daily load;
And every care is pillowed there
  Upon the thought of God.

I ask not far before to see,
  But take in trust my road;
Life, death, and immortality
  Are in my thought of God.

To this their secret strength they owed
  The martyr's path who trod;
The fountains of their patience flowed
  From out their thought of God.

Be still the light upon my way,
  My pilgrim staff and rod,
My rest by night, my strength by day,
  O blessèd thought of God.

*F. L. Hosmer**

79

Farrant C.M.

O NAME, all other names above,
What art thou not to me,
Now I have learned to trust thy love
And cast my care on thee!

What is our being but a cry,
A restless longing still,
Which thou alone canst satisfy,
Alone thy fulness fill!

Thrice blessèd be the holy souls
That lead the way to thee,
That burn upon the martyr-rolls
And lists of prophecy.

And good it is to tread the ground
O'er which their faith hath trod;
But better far, when thou art found,
The soul's own sense of God.

The thought of thee all sorrow calms,
Our anxious burdens fall;
Their crosses turn to triumph-palms
Who find in God their all.

*F. L. Hosmer**

80

University College 77.77.

LIFE of Ages, richly poured,
Love of God, unspent and free,
Flowing in the prophet's word,
And the people's liberty!

Never was to chosen race
That unstinted tide confined;
Thine is every time and place,
Fountain sweet of heart and mind:

Breathing in the thinker's creed,
Pulsing in the martyr's blood,
Nerving simplest thought and deed,
Freshening time with truth and good;

Consecrating art and song,
Holy book and pilgrim track,
Hurling floods of tyrant wrong
From the sacred limits back!

Life of Ages richly poured,
Love of God unspent and free,
Flow still in the prophet's word,
And the people's liberty!

*S. Johnson**

81

Wiltshire C.M.

O THOU, in all thy might so far,
In all thy love so near,
Beyond the range of sun and star,
And yet beside us here,

What heart can comprehend thy Name
Or, searching, find thee out,
Who art within, a quickening flame,
A presence round about?

Yet though I know thee but in part,
I ask not, Lord, for more:
Enough for me to know thou art,
To love thee and adore.

Oh, deeper than aught else besides,
The tender mystery
That like a veil of shadow hides
The Light I may not see!

And dearer than all things I know
Is childlike faith to me,
That makes the darkest way I go
An open path to thee.

*F. L. Hosmer**

82

Erfurt *886.886.*

LORD God, by whom all change is wrought,
By whom new things to birth are brought,
  In whom no change is known!
Whate'er thou dost, whate'er thou art,
Thy people still in thee have part;
  Still, still thou art our own.

Ancient of Days! we dwell in thee;
Out of thine own eternity
  Our peace and joy are wrought;
We rest in our eternal God,
And make secure and safe abode
  With thee, who changest not.

Spirit who makest all things new,
Thou leadest onward; we pursue
  The heavenly march sublime.
'Neath thy renewing fire we glow,
And still from strength to strength we go,
  From height to height we climb.

Darkness and dread we leave behind;
New light, new glory still we find,
  New realms divine possess;
New births of grace, new raptures bring;
Triumphant, the new song we sing,
  The great Renewer bless.

To thee we rise, in thee we rest;
We stay at home, we go in quest,
  Still thou art our abode.
The rapture swells, the wonder grows,
As full on us new life still flows
  From our unchanging God.

*T. H. Gill**

83

Morning Hymn *L.M.*

O GOD, in whom we live and move,
Thy love is law, thy law is love;
Thy present Spirit waits to fill
The soul which comes to do thy will.

Unto thy children's spirits teach
Thy love, beyond the power of speech;
And make them know, with joyful awe,
The encircling presence of thy law.

That law doth give to truth and right,
Howe'er despised, a conquering might,
And makes each fondly cherished lie,
And boasting wrong, to cower and die.

Its patient working doth fulfil
Our hope, and thy all-perfect will;
Nor suffers one true word or thought
Or deed of love, to come to nought.

Such faith, O God, our spirits fill
That we may work in patience still;
Who works for justice, works with thee,
Who works in love, thy child shall be.

*S. Longfellow**

84

Bishopthorpe *C.M.*

IMMORTAL Love, for ever full,
For ever flowing free,
For ever shared, for ever whole,
A never-ebbing sea!

Our outward lips confess the Name
All other names above;
Love only knoweth whence it came,
And comprehendeth love.

Blow, winds of God, awake and blow
The mists of earth away;
Shine out, O Light divine, and show
How wide and far we stray.

The letter fails, the systems fall,
And every symbol wanes;
The Spirit over-brooding all,
Eternal Love, remains.

J. G. Whittier

85

Rivaulx L.M.

O LOVE divine, that stoop'st to share
Our sharpest pang, our bitterest tear,
On thee we cast each earth-born care;
We smile at pain while thou art near.

Though long the weary way we tread,
And sorrow crown each lingering year,
No path we shun, no darkness dread,
Our hearts still whispering, thou art near.

When drooping pleasure turns to grief,
And trembling faith is changed to fear,
The murmuring wind, the quivering leaf,
Shall softly tell us, thou art near.

On thee we cast our burdening woe,
O Love divine, for ever dear;
Content to suffer, while we know,
Living and dying, thou art near.

O. W. Holmes

86

Crimond C.M.

THE Lord's my Shepherd, I'll not want,
He makes me down to lie
In pastures green, he leadeth me
The quiet waters by.

My soul he doth restore again;
  And me to walk doth make
Within the paths of righteousness,
  E'en for his own name's sake.

Yea, though I walk in death's dark vale,
  Yet will I fear no ill;
For thou art with me, and thy rod
  And staff me comfort still.

My table thou has furnishèd
  In presence of my foes;
My head thou dost with oil anoint,
  And my cup overflows.

Goodness and mercy all my life
  Shall surely follow me;
And in God's house for evermore
  My dwelling-place shall be.

Scottish Psalter

87

St. Columba 87.87.(iambic)

THE King of love my Shepherd is,
  Whose goodness faileth never;
I nothing lack if I am his,
  And he is mine for ever.

Where streams of living water flow
  My ransomed soul he leadeth,
And where the verdant pastures grow
  With food celestial feedeth.

Perverse and foolish oft I strayed,
  But yet in love he sought me,
And on his shoulder gently laid,
  And home, rejoicing, brought me.

In death's dark vale I fear no ill
  With thee, dear Lord, beside me;
Thy rod and staff my comfort still,
  Thy Light before to guide me.

Thou spread'st a table in my sight;
Thy unction grace bestoweth;
And, oh, what transport of delight
From thy pure chalice floweth!

And so through all the length of days
Thy goodness faileth never;
Good Shepherd, may I sing thy praise
Within thy house for ever.

*Sir Henry Williams Baker**

88

Surrey 88.88.88.

THE Lord my pasture shall prepare,
And feed me with a shepherd's care;
His presence shall my wants supply,
And guard me with a watchful eye;
My noonday walks he shall attend,
And all my midnight hours defend.

When in the sultry glebe I faint,
Or on the thirsty mountain pant,
To fertile vales and dewy meads
My weary wand'ring steps he leads,
Where peaceful rivers, soft and slow,
Amid the verdant landscape flow.

Though in a bare and rugged way,
Through devious, lonely wilds I stray,
Thy bounty shall my pains beguile;
The barren wilderness shall smile,
With sudden green and herbage crowned,
And streams shall murmur all around.

Though in the paths of death I tread,
With gloomy horrors overspread,
My steadfast heart shall fear no ill,
For thou, O Lord, art with me still:
Thy friendly crook shall give me aid,
And guide me through the dreadful shade.

Joseph Addison

89

Gonfalon Royal L.M.

O LOVE divine! whose constant beam
Shines on the eyes that will not see,
And waits to bless us, while we dream
Thou leav'st us when we turn from thee!

All souls that struggle and aspire,
All hearts of prayer by thee are lit;
And, dim or clear, thy tongues of fire
On distant tribes and centuries sit.

Truth which the sage and prophet saw,
Long sought without, but found within –
The Law of Love beyond all law,
The Life o'erflooding death and sin.

Shine, light of God! make broad thy scope
To all who sin and suffer; more
And better than we dare to hope,
Make with thy love our longings poor.

*J. G. Whittier**

90

Laus Deo 87.87.

GOD is love: his mercy brightens
All the path in which we rove;
Bliss he wakes, and woe he lightens;
God is wisdom, God is love.

Chance and change are busy ever,
We decay and ages move;
But his mercy waneth never;
God is wisdom, God is love.

E'en the hour that darkest seemeth
Will his changeless goodness prove;
From the mist his brightness streameth;
God is wisdom, God is love.

He with earthly cares entwineth
   Hope and comfort from above;
Everywhere his glory shineth;
   God is wisdom, God is love.

*Sir John Bowring**

91

Strength and Stay 11 10.11 10.

FATHER, in thy mysterious presence kneeling,
   Gladly our souls would feel thy kindling love;
For we are weak and need some deep revealing
   Of trust, and strength, and calmness from above.

Lord, we have wandered forth through doubt and sorrow,
   And thou hast made each step an onward one;
And we will ever trust each unknown morrow:
   Thou wilt sustain us till its work is done.

In the heart's depth a peace serene and holy
   Abides; and when pain seems to have its will,
Or we despair, oh, may that peace rise slowly,
   Stronger than agony, and we be still!

Now, Father, now, in thy dear presence kneeling,
   Our spirits yearn to feel thy kindling love;
Now make us strong: we need thy deep revealing
   Of trust, and strength, and calmness from above.

S. Johnson

92

Stracathro C.M.

THOU Grace divine, encircling all,
   A shoreless, soundless sea,
Wherein at last our souls must fall,
   O Love of God most free!

When over dizzy heights we go,
   One soft hand blinds our eyes,
The other leads us safe and slow,
   O Love of God most wise!

And though we turn us from thy face,
  And wander wide and long,
Thou hold'st us still in thine embrace,
  O Love of God most strong!

The saddened heart, the restless soul,
  The toil-worn frame and mind,
Alike confess thy sure control,
  O Love of God most kind!

And filled and quickened by thy breath,
  Our souls are strong and free
To rise o'er sin, and fear, and death,
  O Love of God, to thee!

*Eliza Scudder**

93

Cross of Jesus 87.87.

THERE'S a wideness in God's mercy
  Like the wideness of the sea;
There's a kindness in his justice
  Which is more than liberty.

There is no place where earth's sorrows
  Are more felt than up in heaven;
There is no place where earth's failings
  Have such kindly judgment given.

For the love of God is broader
  Than the measures of our mind,
And the heart of the Eternal
  Is most wonderfully kind.

But we make his love too narrow
  By false limits of our own,
And we magnify his strictness
  With a zeal he will not own.

If our love were but more simple,
  We should take him at his word,
And our lives would be all glorious
  In the radiance of our Lord.

*F. W. Faber**

94

St Bernard C.M.

THE Lord is in his Holy Place
  In all things near and far;
The beauty of the snow-flake, he,
  And glory of the star.

Our art may build its house of God,
  Our feet on Sinai stand;
But Holiest of Holies knows
  No tread, no touch of hand.

He hides himself within the love
  Of those whom we love best;
The smiles and tones that makes our homes
  Are shrines by him possessed.

He tents within the lonely heart,
  And shepherds every thought;
We find him not by seeking long;
  We lose him not, unsought.

The listening soul makes Sinai still
  Wherever we may be,
And in the vow, "Thy will be done,"
  Lies all Gethsemane.

Oh, everywhere his Holy Place
  If love unseal the eyes,
And everywhere the waiting Face
  To welcome and surprise!

*W. C. Gannett**

95

Salzburg 77.77.D.

O ETERNAL Life, whose power
  Gathers ages to a span;
From whose being breaks the flower,
From whose love our life began;
By the whisper of whose breath
Atoms wake that seem but death;
With whose silent-working will
The eternal ages thrill!

Lord of life, to heaven tower
Spires of being high and grand,
Till on us thou lay the power
That we serve with heart and hand;
Till thou flood us with thy light,
That we see thee with our sight,
Who art Reason, who art Right,
Majesty of Love and Might!

Not on earth the glory ends;
In unnumbered worlds it reigns;
From eternity descends,
To eternity remains.
When the things we hear and see
Vanish in life's mystery,
Still all glories that can be
Wait in thine infinity.

*J. V. Blake**

96

Kilmarnock C.M.

FATHER, by whatsoever light
Our path of life we see,
It matters not, so at the last
It leadeth us to thee.

We thank thee for the star that rose
O'er old Judaea bright;
And that its deathless ray still shines,
To fill our souls with light.

We thank thee, too, that other stars
O'er other lands have shone,
To guide the stumbling feet of those
Who toward thee struggle on.

Thou many names of saving power
Hast given to us, then;
And each new truth that lifts the world
Is God come down again.

*M. J. Savage**

97

Kent L.M.

HOW happy are they born or taught,
Who do not serve another's will;
Whose armour is their honest thought,
And simple truth their highest skill;

Whose passions not their rulers are;
Whose souls are still, and free from fear,
Not tied unto the world with care
Of public fame or private ear;

Who God doth late and early pray
That more of grace than goods he lends;
And walk with all, from day to day,
As with their neighbours and their friends.

All such are freed from servile bands
Of hope to rise, or fear to fall;
They rule themselves, but rule not lands,
And, having nothing, yet have all.

Sir Henry Wotton (altered)

98

Christus der ist mein Leben 76.76.

THE light pours down from heaven,
And enters where it may;
The eyes of all earth's children
Are cheered with one bright ray.

So let the mind's true sunshine
Be spread o'er earth as free,
And fill our waiting spirits
As the waters fill the sea.

The soul can shed a glory
On every work well done,
As even things most lowly
Are radiant in the sun.

Then let each human spirit
Enjoy the vision bright;
The truth which comes from heaven
Shall spread like heaven's own light;

Till earth becomes God's temple,
And every human heart
Shall join in one great service,
Each happy in its part.

*J. Gostick**

99

Lux Eoi 87.87.D.

LIGHT of ages and of nations!
Every race and every time
Hath received thine inspirations,
Glimpses of thy truth sublime.
Ever spirits, in rapt vision,
Passed the heavenly veil within;
Ever hearts, bowed in contrition,
Found salvation from their sin.

Reason's noble aspiration
Truth in growing clearness saw;
Conscience spoke its condemnation,
Or proclaimed the eternal Law.
While thine inward revelations
Told thy saints their prayers were heard,
Prophets to the guilty nations
Spoke thine everlasting word.

Lord, that word abideth ever;
Revelation is not sealed;
Answering unto our endeavour,
Truth and right are still revealed.
That which came to ancient sages,
Greek, Barbarian, Roman, Jew,
Written in the heart's deep pages,
Shines to-day, for ever new!

*S. Longfellow**

100

Farmer/Moscow 664.6664.

COME, Holy One, in love;
Shed on us from above
Thine own bright ray;
Divinely good thou art;
Thy sacred gifts impart
To gladden each sad heart,
O come to-day!

Come, truest Friend and best,
Our most delightful guest,
With soothing power:
Rest which the weary know,
Shade 'mid the noontide glow,
Peace when deep griefs o'erflow,
Cheer us this hour!

Come, Light serene and still,
Our inmost bosoms fill;
Dwell in each breast;
We know no dawn but thine;
Send forth thy beams divine
On our dark souls to shine,
And make us blest.

Exalt our low desires;
Extinguish passion's fires;
Heal every wound;
Our stubborn spirits bend;
Our icy coldness end;
Our devious steps attend,
While heavenward bound.

Latin Hymn, trans. R. Palmer

101

Caithness C.M.

WISDOM hath treasures greater far
Than east or west unfold,
And her rewards more precious are
Than is the gain of gold.

In her right hand she holds to view
  A length of happy years,
And in her left the prize of fame
  And honour bright appears.

She guides the young with innocence
  In pleasure's path to tread;
A crown of glory she bestows
  Upon the hoary head.

According as her labours rise,
  So her rewards increase;
Her ways are ways of pleasantness,
  And all her paths are peace.

Scottish Paraphrases

102

Franconia S.M.

BLEST are the pure in heart,
  For they shall see our God;
The secret of the Lord is theirs;
  Their soul is God's abode.

Still to the lowly soul
  He doth himself impart,
And for his dwelling and his throne
  Chooseth the pure in heart.

Lord, we thy presence seek;
  May ours this blessing be:
Give us a pure and lowly heart,
  A temple meet for thee.

John Keble vv.1 and 2
Hall's Psalms and Hymns v.3

103

Abbot's Leigh 87.87. D.

GOD is Love: let heaven adore him;
  God is Love: let earth rejoice;
Let creation sing before him,
  And exalt him with one voice.
He who laid the earth's foundation,
  He who spread the heavens above,
He who breathes through all creation,
He is Love, eternal Love.

God is Love: and he enfoldeth
  All the world in one embrace;
With unfailing grasp he holdeth
  Every child of every race.
And when human hearts are breaking
  Under sorrow's iron rod,
Then they find that selfsame aching
  Deep within the heart of God.

God is Love: and though with blindness
  Sin afflicts our souls again,
God's eternal loving-kindness
  Holds and guides them even then.
Sin and death and hell shall never
  O'er us final triumph gain;
God is Love, so Love for ever
  O'er the universe must reign.

*T. Rees**

104

Dundee C.M.

O THOU, whose nature and whose name
Is heavenly love divine,
Shine into these poor hearts of ours
And make them wholly thine.

We feel unworthy of thy love;
We bow our heads in shame;
Unworthy we to take upon
Our lips thy holy name.

Forgiveness thou wilt not withhold:
Our saviour came to show
The depth of love which in thy heart
For humankind doth glow.

He lived, he died, that we in him
Thy glorious self might see,
Might know the fulness of thy love –
The love that is in thee.

Hush then the anxious, troubled heart;
From doubts and fears set free;
Forgiveness, peace, joy, holiness,
Are ours, O Lord, in thee.

Jamie A. Smith

105

Quem Pastores 888.7.

LIKE a mighty river flowing,
Like a flower in beauty growing,
Far beyond all human knowing
Is the perfect peace of God.

Like the hills serene and even,
Like the coursing clouds of heaven,
Like the heart that's been forgiven
Is the perfect peace of God.

Like the summer breezes playing,
Like the tall trees softly swaying,
Like the lips of silent praying
Is the perfect peace of God.

Like the morning sun ascended,
Like the scents of evening blended,
Like a friendship never ended
Is the perfect peace of God.

Like the azure ocean swelling,
Like the jewel all-excelling,
Far beyond our human telling
 Is the perfect peace of God.

Michael Perry

106

Ravenshaw 66.66.

LORD, thy word abideth,
And our footsteps guideth;
Who its truth believeth
Light and joy receiveth.

When our foes are near us,
Then thy word doth cheer us:
Word of consolation,
Message of salvation.

When the storms are o'er us
And dark clouds before us,
Then its light directeth,
And our way protecteth.

Who can tell the pleasure,
Who recount the treasure,
By thy word imparted
To the simple-hearted?

Word of mercy, giving
Succour to the living;
Word of life, supplying
Comfort to the dying!

O that we, discerning
Its most holy learning,
Lord, may love, revere thee,
Evermore be near thee.

*Sir Henry Williams Baker**

107

Bristol C.M.

HARK the glad sound! the saviour comes,
The saviour promised long!
Let every heart prepare a throne,
And every voice a song.

On him the Spirit, largely poured,
Exerts its sacred fire,
Wisdom and might and zeal and love,
His holy breast inspire.

He comes the prisoners to release,
In Satan's bondage held:
The gates of brass before him burst,
The iron fetters yield.

He comes the broken heart to bind,
The bleeding soul to cure,
And with the treasures of his grace
To enrich the humble poor.

Our glad hosannas, Prince of Peace,
Thy welcome shall proclaim;
And heaven's eternal arches ring
With thy belovèd name.

Philip Doddridge

108

Cambridge S.M.

HOW beauteous are their feet,
Who stand on Zion's hill!
Who bring salvation on their tongues,
And words of peace reveal!

How happy are our ears,
That hear the joyful sound,
Which kings and prophets waited for,
And sought but never found.

How blessèd are our eyes,
That see the heav'nly light;
Prophets and kings desired it long,
But died without the sight.

And we as they desire
What those to come shall see.
In truth and peace shall they rejoice,
Yea, happy shall they be.

We stand on Zion's hill;
Christ doth our song inspire
To hail the day that shall fulfil
The joy of our desire.

*Isaac Watts and R. Bridges**

109

Deo Gracias 88.88.88.

LIFT up your heads, ye mighty gates,
Behold, the King of glory waits,
The Prince of Peace is drawing near,
The hope of longing hearts is here;
The end of all our woe he brings,
Wherefore the earth is glad and sings.

Oh, blest the land, the city blest,
Where Christ the ruler is confessed!
Oh, happy hearts and happy homes
To whom this King in triumph comes!
His kingly crown is holiness,
His sceptre, pity in distress.

Fling wide the portals of your heart,
Make it a temple set apart
From earthly use for heaven's employ,
Adorned with prayer, and love, and joy;
So shall your sovereign enter in,
And new and nobler life begin.

*G. Weissel, trans. Catherine Winkworth**

110

Cross of Jesus 87.87.

COME, thou long-expected Jesus,
Born to set thy people free,
From our fears and sins release us,
Let us find our rest in thee.

Israel's strength and consolation,
Hope of all the earth thou art,
Dear desire of every nation,
Joy of every longing heart.

Born thy people to deliver,
Born a child and yet a king,
Born to reign in us for ever,
Now thy gracious kingdom bring.

By thine own eternal Spirit
Rule in all our hearts alone;
By thine all-sufficient merit
Raise us to thy glorious throne.

Charles Wesley

111

Our God Reigns *Irregular*

HOW lovely on the mountains are the feet of him
Who brings good news, good news.
Proclaiming peace, announcing news of happiness,
Our God reigns, our God reigns, our God reigns,
Our God reigns, our God reigns, our God reigns!

You watchmen lift your voices joyfully as one.
Shout for your King, your King.
See eye to eye the Lord restoring Zion:
Your God reigns, your God reigns, your God reigns,
Your God reigns, your God reigns, your God reigns!

Waste places of Jerusalem break forth with joy,
We are redeemed, redeemed.
The Lord has saved and comforted his people:
Your God reigns, your God reigns, your God reigns,
Your God reigns, your God reigns, your God reigns!

Ends of the earth, see the salvation of your God.
Jesus is Lord, is Lord.
Before the nations he has bared his holy arm:
Your God reigns, your God reigns, your God reigns,
Your God reigns, your God reigns, your God reigns!

Leonard E. Smith Jnr.

112

Veni Emmanuel 88.88.88.

O COME, O come, Immanuel,
And ransom captive Israel,
That mourns in lonely exile here
Until the Son of God appear:
Rejoice! Rejoice! Immanuel
Shall come to thee, O Israel.

O come, O come, thou Lord of might,
Who to thy tribes, on Sinai's height,
In ancient times didst give the law
In cloud, and majesty, and awe:

O come, thou Rod of Jesse, free
Thine own from Satan's tyranny;
From depths of hell thy people save,
And give them vict'ry o'er the grave:

O come, thou Key of David, come,
And open wide our heav'nly home;
Make safe the way that leads on high,
And close the path to misery:

O come, thou Day-spring, come and cheer
Our spirits by thine advent here;
Disperse the gloomy clouds of night,
And death's dark shadows put to flight:

18th Century Latin
trans. J. M. Neale and others

113

Little Cornard 66.66.88.

HILLS of the north, rejoice,
River and mountain-spring,
Hark to the advent voice;
Valley and lowland, sing.
Though absent long, your Lord is nigh;
He judgment brings and victory.

Isles of southern seas,
Sing to the listening earth;
Carry on every breeze
Hope of a world's new birth:
In Christ shall all be made anew;
His word is sure, his promise true.

Lands of the east, arise!
He is your brightest morn;
Greet him with joyous eyes,
Let praise his path adorn:
Your seers have longed to know their Lord:
To you he comes, the final Word.

Shores of the utmost west,
Lands of the setting sun,
Welcome the heavenly guest
In whom the dawn has come:
He brings a never-ending light,
Who triumphed o'er our darkest night.

Shout, while you journey home;
Songs be in every mouth!
Lo, from the north we come,
From east and west and south:
City of God, the bond are free,
We come to live and reign in thee!

C. E. Oakley and editors of English Praise (1975)*

114

Winchester Old C.M.

WHILE shepherds watched their flocks by night,
All seated on the ground,
The angel of Lord came down,
And glory shone around.

"Fear not," said he (for mighty dread
Had seized their troubled mind),
"Glad tidings of great joy I bring
To you and all mankind.

"To you, in David's town, this day
Is born of David's line
A saviour, who is Christ the Lord;
And this shall be the sign:

"The heavenly babe you there shall find
To human view displayed,
All meanly wrapped in swaddling bands,
And in a manger laid."

Thus spake the seraph; and forthwith
Appeared a shining throng
Of angels, praising God, and thus
Addressed their joyful song:

"All glory be to God on high,
And to the earth be peace;
Goodwill henceforth from heaven to men
Begin, and never cease!"

N. Tate

115

Cranham 65.65.D.

IN the lonely midnight,
On the wintry hill,
Shepherds heard the angels,
Singing, "Peace, goodwill."
Listen, O ye weary,
To the angels' song,
Unto you the tidings
Of great joy belong.

Though in David's city
Angels sing no more,
Love makes angel music
On earth's darkest shore;
Though no heavenly glory
Meet your wondering eyes,
Love can make your dwelling
Bright as Paradise.

Though the child of Mary
Sent from heaven on high,
In his manger cradle
May no longer lie,
Love is king forever,
Though the proud world scorn;
If ye truly seek him,
Christ your King is born .

T. C. Williams

116

Stille Nacht Irregular

SILENT night! peaceful night!
All things sleep, shepherds keep
Watch on Bethlehem's silent hill,
And unseen, while all is still,
Angels watch above.

Bright the star shines afar,
Guiding travellers on their way;
Who their gold and incense bring,
Offerings to the promised king,
  Child of David's line.

Light around! joyous sound!
Angel voices wake the air;
Glory be to God in heaven,
Peace on earth to you is given;
  Lo! the Christ is born!

J. Mohr

117

Forest Green/Christmas Carol C.M.D.

O LITTLE town of Bethlehem,
How still we see thee lie!
Above thy deep and dreamless sleep
  The silent stars go by.
Yet in thy dark streets shineth
  The everlasting light;
The hopes and fears of all the years
  Are met in thee to-night.

O morning stars, together
  Proclaim the holy birth,
And praises sing to God the King,
  And peace to all on earth;
For Christ is born of Mary;
  And, gathered all above,
While mortals sleep, the angels keep
  Their watch of wondering love.

How silently, how silently,
  The wondrous gift is given!
So God imparts to human hearts
  The blessings of his heaven.
No ear may hear his coming;
  But in this world of sin,
Where meek souls will receive him, still
  The dear Christ enters in.

Where children pure and happy
 Pray to the blessed child,
Where misery cries out to thee,
 Son of the mother mild;
Where charity stands watching
 And faith holds wide the door,
The dark night wakes,the glory breaks,
 And Christmas comes once more.

O holy Child of Bethlehem,
 Descend to us, we pray;
Cast out our sin, and enter in,
 Be born in us to-day.
We hear the Christmas angels
 The great glad tidings tell:
O come to us, abide with us,
 Our Lord Emmanuel.

*P. Brooks**

118

The First Nowell *Irregular*

THE first Nowell the angel did say
Was to certain poor shepherds in fields as they lay;
In fields where they lay keeping their sheep,
On a cold winter's night that was so deep,
 Nowell, Nowell, Nowell, Nowell,
 Born is the King of Israel.

They lookèd, up and saw a star
Shining in the east, beyond them far,
And to the earth it gave great light,
And so it continued both day and night.

And by the light of that same star
Three wise men came from country far;
To seek for a king was their intent
And to follow the star wherever it went.

This star drew nigh to the north-west;
O'er Bethlehem it took its rest,
And there it did both stop and stay,
Right over the place where Jesus lay.

Then entered in those wise men three,
Full reverently upon their knee,
And offered there, in his presence,
Both gold and myrrh and frankincense.

Carol (traditional)

119

Adeste fideles *Irregular*

O COME, all ye faithful,
Joyful and triumphant,
O come ye, O come ye to Bethlehem:
Come and behold him
Born this happy morning:
O come, let us adore him,
O come, let us adore him,
O come, let us adore him,
Christ, the Lord.

See how the shepherds,
Summoned to his cradle,
Leaving their flocks draw nigh with lowly fear;
We too will thither
Bend our joyful footsteps:

Lo, star-led chieftains,
Wise men, Christ adoring,
Offer him incense, gold and myrrh;
We to the Christ-child
Bring our hearts' oblations:

Sing, choirs of angels,
Sing in exultation,
Sing, all ye citizens of heaven above;
Glory to God
In the highest:

*Latin 18th Cent., trans. F. Oakeley**

120

Mendelssohn 77.77. D. with refrain

HARK! the herald angels sing
Glory to the new-born King:
Peace on earth and mercy mild
God and sinners reconciled.
Joyful, all ye nations rise,
Join the triumph of the skies;
With the angelic host proclaim,
"Christ is born in Bethlehem."
Hark! the herald angels sing
Glory to the new-born King.

Hail! the holy Prince of Peace!
Hail, the Sun of righteousness!
Light and life to all he brings,
Comes with healing in his wings.
Joyful, all ye nations, rise,
Join the triumph of the skies;
With the angelic host proclaim,
"Christ is born in Bethlehem".
Hark! the herald angels sing
Glory to the new-born King.

*Charles Wesley**

121

In dulci jubilo Irregular

GOOD Christian folk rejoice
With heart, and soul, and voice;
Give ye heed to what we say:
Jesus Christ is born today;
Ox and ass before him bow;
He is in the manger now.
Christ is born to-day!

Good Christian folk rejoice
  With heart, and soul, and voice;
Tidings hear of fullest bliss:
  Jesus Christ was born for this;
Unto you both way and door –
  Life and light for evermore.
Christ was born for this!

Good Christian folk rejoice
  With heart, and soul, and voice;
Lo, the message which ye crave:
  Jesus Christ was born to save!
Born to bring to all good-will,
  Fainting hearts with hope to fill.
Christ was born to save!

*trans. J. M. Neale**

122

Noel C.M.D.

IT came upon the midnight clear,
  That glorious song of old,
From angels bending near the earth
  To touch their harps of gold:
"Peace to the earth, goodwill to men
  From heaven's all-gracious King!"
The world in solemn stillness lay
  To hear the angels sing.

Still through the cloven skies they come,
  With peaceful wings unfurled;
And still their heavenly music floats
  O'er all the weary world.
Above its sad and lowly plains
  They bend, on hovering wing,
And ever o'er its Babel sounds
  The blessèd angels sing.

Yet with the woes of sin and strife
The world has suffered long:
Beneath the angel-strain have rolled
Two thousand years of wrong;
And man, at war with man, hears not
The love-song which they bring:
O hush the noise, ye men of strife,
And hear the angels sing!

And ye, beneath life's crushing load
Whose forms are bending low,
Who toil along the climbing way
With painful steps and slow;
Look now! for glad and golden hours
Come swiftly on the wing;
O rest beside the weary road,
And hear the angels sing!

For lo! the days are hastening on,
By prophet-bards foretold,
When, with the ever-circling years,
Comes round the age of gold;
When peace shall over all the earth
Its ancient splendours fling,
And the whole world send back the song
Which now the angels sing.

E. H. Sears

123

St.Stephen C.M.

TO-DAY be joy in every heart,
For lo, the angel throng
Once more above the listening earth
Repeats the advent song:

"Peace on the earth, goodwill to men!"
Before us goes the star,
That leads us on to holier births
And life diviner far.

Ye men of strife, forget to-day
  Your harshness and your hate;
Too long ye stay the promised years
  For which the nations wait.

And ye upon the tented field,
  Sheathe, sheathe to-day the sword;
By love, and not by might, shall come
  The kingdom of the Lord.

O star of human faith and hope,
  Thy light shall lead us on,
Until it fades in morning's glow,
  And heaven on earth is won!

F. L. Hosmer

124

Church Triumphant L.M.

I HEARD the bells on Christmas Day
Their old familiar carols play,
  And wild and sweet
  The words repeat,
Of "Peace on earth, goodwill to men!"

I thought how, as the day had come,
The belfries of all Christendom
  Had rolled along
  The unbroken song,
Of "Peace on earth, goodwill to men!"

Till ringing, singing on its way,
The world revolved from night to day,
  A voice, a chime,
  A chant sublime,
Of "Peace on earth, goodwill to men!"

And in despair I bowed my head;
"There is no peace on earth," I said.
  "For hate is strong
  And mocks the song
Of Peace on earth, goodwill to men!"

Then pealed the bells more loud and deep:
"God is not dead; nor doth he sleep!
The wrong shall fail,
The right prevail,
With Peace on earth, goodwill to men!"

H. W. Longfellow

125

Nativity C.M.

LONG, long ago, in manger low
Was cradled from above
A little Child, in whom God smiled,
A Christmas gift of love.

When hearts were bitter and unjust,
And cruel hands were strong,
The noise he hushed with hope and trust,
And Peace began her song.

Whene'er the Father's Christmas gifts
Seem only frost and snow,
And anxious stress and loneliness
And poverty and woe;

Straightway provide a welcome wide,
Nor wonder why they came;
They stand outside our hearts and bide,
Knocking in Jesus' name.

For trouble, cold, and dreary care
Are angels in disguise;
And greeted fair, with trust and prayer,
As peace and love they rise!

They are the manger rude and low,
In which a Christ-child lies;
O welcome guest, thy cradle nest
Is always God's surprise!

Jane Andrews and W. C. Gannett

126

Peterborough L.M.D.

THE Lord is come! On Syrian soil
The child of poverty and toil;
The man of Sorrows, born to know
Each varying shade of human woe;
His joy, his glory, to fulfil,
In earth and heaven, his Father's will;
On lonely mount, by festive board,
On bitter cross, despised, adored.

The Lord is come! Dull hearts to wake,
He speaks, as never man yet spake,
The truth which makes his servants free,
The royal law of liberty.
Though heaven and earth shall pass away,
His living words our spirits stay,
And from his treasures, new and old
The eternal mysteries unfold.

The Lord is come! In every heart
Where truth and mercy claim a part;
In every land where right is might,
And deeds of darkness shun the light;
In every church where faith and love
Lift earthward thoughts to things above;
In every holy, happy home,
We bless thee, Lord, that thou hast come.

A. P. Stanley

127

Branle de l' Official 77.77.10.10.

DING dong! merrily on high
In heav'n the bells are ringing:
Ding dong! verily the sky
Is riv'n with angel singing.
Gloria, Hosanna in excelsis!
Gloria, Hosanna in excelsis!

E'en so here below, below,
Let steeple bells be swungen,
And i-o, i-o, i-o,
By priest and people sungen.

Pray you, dutifully prime
Your matin chime, ye ringers;
May you beautifully rime
Your eve-time song, ye singers.

G. R. Woodward

128

Antioch 86.8.668.

JOY to the world, the Lord is come!
Let earth receive her King;
Let every heart prepare him room,
And heaven and nature sing,
And heaven and nature sing,
And heaven, and heaven and nature sing.

Joy to the world, the saviour reigns!
Let all their songs employ;
While fields and floods, rocks, hills and plains
Repeat the sounding joy,
Repeat the sounding joy,
Repeat, repeat the sounding joy.

He rules the world with truth and grace,
And makes the nations prove
The glories of his righteousness
And wonders of his love,
And wonders of his love,
And wonders, wonders of his love.

Isaac Watts

129

Epiphany Hymn *11.10.11.10. (dactylic)*

BRIGHTEST and best of the sons of the morning,
Dawn on our darkness, and lend us thine aid;
Star of the east, the horizon adorning,
Guide where our infant Messiah is laid.

Cold on his cradle the dew-drops are shining;
Low lies his head with the beasts of the stall;
Angels adore him in slumber reclining,
Son of our Father and brother of all.

Say, shall we yield him, in costly devotion,
Odours of Edom, and offerings divine,
Gems of the mountain and pearls of the ocean,
Myrrh from the forest or gold from the mine?

Vainly we offer each ample oblation;
Vainly with gifts would his favour secure;
Richer by far is the heart's adoration;
Dearer to God are the prayers of the poor.

Brightest and best of the sons of the morning,
Dawn on our darkness, and lend us thine aid;
Star of the east, the horizon adorning,
Guide where our infant Messiah is laid.

*R.Heber**

130

Every star shall sing a carol *87.87.66.*

EVERY star shall sing a carol;
Every creature, high or low,
Come and praise the King of Heaven
By whatever name you know:
God above, Man below,
Holy is the name I know.

When the King of all creation
Had a cradle on the earth,
Holy was the human body,
Holy was the human birth:

Who can tell what other cradle,
  High above the Milky Way,
Still may rock the King of Heaven
  On another Christmas Day?

Who can count how many crosses,
  Still to come or long ago,
Crucify the King of Heaven?
  Holy is the name I know:

Who can tell what other body
  He will hallow for his own?
I will praise the son of Mary,
  Brother of my blood and bone:

Every star and every planet,
  Every creature, high or low,
Come and praise the King of Heaven
  By whatever name you know:

Sydney Carter

131

Irby 87.87.77.

ONCE in royal David's city
  Stood a lowly cattle-shed,
Where a mother laid her baby
  In a manger for his bed:
Mary was that mother mild,
Jesus Christ her little child.

Since he shared our human nature,
  Day by day like us he grew,
He was little, weak, and helpless,
  Tears and smiles like us he knew;
And he feeleth for our sadness,
And he shareth in our gladness.

And our eyes at last shall see him,
  Through his own redeeming love,
For that child so dear and gentle
  Is our Lord in heaven above:
And he leads his children on
To the place where he is gone.

Not in that poor lowly stable,
With the oxen standing by,
We shall see him; but in heaven,
Set at God's right hand on high;
When like stars his children crowned
All in white shall wait around.

*Cecil Frances Alexander**

132

Away in a manger *11 11. 11 11.*

AWAY in a manger, no crib for a bed,
The little Lord Jesus laid down his sweet head;
The stars in the bright sky looked down where he lay,
The little Lord Jesus asleep on the hay.

The cattle are lowing, the baby awakes,
But little Lord Jesus no crying he makes.
I love thee, Lord Jesus! Look down from the sky,
And stay by my side until morning is nigh.

Be near me, Lord Jesus; I ask thee to stay
Close by me for ever, and love me, I pray.
Bless all the dear children in thy tender care,
And fit us for heaven, to live with thee there.

Anon.

133

Child of Joy *Irregular*

O COME this joyous morning to greet a new hope dawning;
A babe to lowly Mary's born – Joy! Joy! Joy!
Come child of joy amongst us;
O child of joy within.

Bells on high are ringing! What gifts shall we be bringing?
O give the greatest gift of all – Love! Love! Love!
Come child of love amongst us;
O child of love within.

Above the night wind sighing hear Mary's babe a-crying
For all the hungry and oppressed – Heed! Heed! Heed!
O child of caring wake us,
O wake us from within.

Rekindle now the chalice bright, and shed around its
golden light;
For by its flame the world shall find – Truth! Truth! Truth!
Come child of light amongst us;
O light of truth within.

O grant to us that we may give to all the right freely to
live.
Yes! colour, culture, creed and tongue – Free! Free! Free!
Come child of joy amongst us,
Thy freedom be within.

O child of sorrow, child of mirth; O child of plenty,
child of dearth,
Awake the dawn that we may see – Light! Light! Light!
Come child of light amongst us;
O Light of God within.

John Elliott

134

Tempus Adest Flor 76.76.D.

GOOD King Wenceslas looked out
On the feast of Stephen.
When the snow lay round about,
Deep, and crisp, and even:
Brightly shone the moon that night,
Though the frost was cruel,
When a poor man came in sight,
Gathering winter fuel.

CHRISTMAS

"Hither, page, and stand by me,
  If thou know'st it, telling,
Yonder peasant, who is he?
  Where and what his dwelling?"
"Sire, he lives a good league hence,
  Underneath the mountain;
Right against the forest fence,
  By Saint Agnes' fountain."

"Bring me flesh, and bring me wine,
  Bring me pine-logs hither;
Thou and I will see him dine,
  When we bear them thither."
Page and monarch forth they went,
  Forth they went together;
Through the rude wind's wild lament.
  And the bitter weather.

"Sire, the night is darker now,
  And the wind blows stronger;
Fails my heart, I know not how,
  I can go no longer."
"Mark my footsteps, good my page,
  Tread thou in them boldly;
Thou shalt find the winter's rage
  Freeze thy blood less coldly."

In his master's steps he trod,
  Where the snow lay dinted;
Heat was in the very sod
  Which the saint had printed.
Therefore, Christian folk, be sure,
  Wealth or rank possessing,
Ye who now will bless the poor
  Shall yourselves find blessing.

*J. M. Neale**

135

Tudor C.M.

IMMORTAL by their deed and word,
Like light around them shed,
Still speak the prophets of the Lord,
Still live the sainted dead.

The voice of old by Jordan's flood
Yet floats upon the air;
We hear it in beatitude,
In parable and prayer.

And still the beauty of that life
Shines star-like on our way;
And breathes its calm amid the strife
And burden of to-day.

Spirit of Jesus, still speed on,
Speed on thy conquering way,
Till every heart the Father own,
And all his will obey!

F. L. Hosmer

136

Kingsfold C.M.D.

WHEN Jesus walked upon the earth
He never talked with kings;
He talked with simple people
Of doing friendly things.
He never praised the conquerors
And all their hero host;
He said the very greatest were
The ones who loved the most.

His words were not of mighty deeds;
But many times he spoke
Of feeding hungry people
And cheering lonely folk.
I'm glad his words were simple words
Just meant for me and you;
The things he asked were simple things
That you and I can do.

*Marion Brown Shelton**

137

Bedford C.M.

CHRIST comes not yet a King to reign,
  The world's long hope is dim;
The weary centuries watch in vain
  The clouds of heaven for him.

But not for signs in heaven above
  Or earth below they look,
Who know with John his smile of love,
  With Peter his rebuke.

In joy of inward peace, or sense
  Of sorrow over sin,
He is his own best evidence,
  His witness is within.

And warm, strong, tender, even yet
  A present help is he;
And faith has still its Olivet,
  And love its Galilee.

The healing of his seamless dress
  Is by our beds of pain;
We touch him in life's throng and press,
  And we are whole again.

O Lord and Master of us all!
  Whate'er our name or sign,
We own thy sway, we hear thy call,
  We test our lives by thine.

*J. G. Whittier**

138

Abridge C.M.

O LORD and Master of us all!
  Whate'er our name or sign,
We own thy sway, we hear thy call,
  We test our lives by thine.

Thou judgest us; thy purity
  Doth all our lusts condemn;
The love that draws us nearer thee
  Is hot with wrath to them.

Yet weak and blinded though we be,
  Thou dost our service own;
We bring our varying gifts to thee,
  And thou rejectest none.

To thee our full humanity,
  Its joys and pains, belong;
The human harm we cause, on thee
  Inflicts a deeper wrong.

O Love! O Life! Our faith and sight
  Thy presence maketh one;
As through transfigured clouds of white
  We trace the noonday sun.

So to our mortal eyes subdued,
  Flesh-veiled, but not concealed,
We know in thee the Fatherhood
  And heart of God revealed.

We faintly hear, we dimly see,
  In differing phrase we pray:
But, dim or clear, we own in thee
  The Light, the Truth, the Way.

*J. G. Whittier**

139

Ellers 10 10.10 10.

O THOU great Friend to all humanity,
Who once appeared in humblest guise below,
Sin to rebuke, to set the captive free,
And call thy people forth from want and woe!

We look to thee; thy truth is still the light
Which guides the nations, groping on their way,
Stumbling and falling in disastrous night,
Yet hoping ever for the perfect day.

Yes! Thou art still the Life; thou art the Way
The holiest know; Light, Life, and Way of heaven!
And they who dearest hope, and deepest pray,
Toil by the light, life, way, which thou hast given.

*Theodore Parker**

140

Glenfinlas 65.65.

WISE men, seeking Jesus,
Travelled from afar,
Guided on their journey
By a beauteous star.

But if we desire him,
He is close at hand;
For our native country
Is our Holy Land.

Prayerful souls may find him
By our quiet lakes,
Meet him on our hillsides
When the morning breaks.

In our fertile cornfields
While the sheaves are bound,
In our busy markets,
Jesus may be found.

Fishermen talk with him
By the great North Sea,
As the first disciples
Did in Galilee.

Every town and village
In our land might be
Made by Jesus' presence
Blest like Bethany.

He is more than near us,
If we love him well;
For he seeketh ever
In our hearts to dwell.

*J. T. East**

141

St. Aelred 888.3

FIERCE raged the tempest o'er the deep,
Watch did thine anxious servants keep;
But thou wast wrapped in guileless sleep,
  Calm and still.

"Save, Lord, we perish!" was their cry,
"O save us in our agony!"
Thy word above the storm rose high:
  "Peace! Be still."

The wild winds hushed; the angry deep
Sank, like a little child, to sleep;
The sullen billows ceased to leap,
  At thy will.

So, when our life is clouded o'er,
And storm-winds drift us from the shore,
Say, lest we sink to rise no more:
  "Peace! Be still."

G. Thring

142

Irish C.M.

O BROTHER of the righteous will,
  O Brother full of grace,
What human glory is revealed,
  Foreshadowed in thy face!

As once the homes of Galilee,
  It lighteth ours to-day;
And still to us it showeth clear
  The Life, the Truth, the Way.

Thou art the Way: for still to know
  The love that reigns above,
There is no other way than thine –
  To live the life of love.

Thou art the Truth: alone on eyes
Like thine the visions fall –
Blessèd, with thee, the pure in heart,
Beholding God in all.

Thou art the Life: in thee we own
The glory all may wear,
Who, one with thee, for truth and right
Will learn to do and dare.

O Brother of the righteous will,
O Brother full of grace,
With deepening love thy faithful ones
Still gaze upon thy face!

*J. W. Chadwick and W. C. Gannett**

143

Nürnberg L.M.

WHERE cross the crowded ways of life,
Where sound the cries of race and clan,
Above the noise of selfish strife,
We hear thy voice, O Son of Man.

In haunts of wretchedness and need,
On shadowed thresholds dark with fears,
From paths where hide the lures of greed,
We catch the vision of thy tears.

From tender childhood's helplessness,
From woman's grief, man's burdened toil,
From famished souls, from sorrow's stress,
Thy heart has never known recoil.

The cup of water given for thee
Still holds the freshness of thy grace;
Yet long these multitudes to see
The full compassion of thy face.

O Master, from the mountain side,
Make haste to heal these hearts of pain;
Among these restless throngs abide,
O tread the city's streets again;

Till everyone shall learn thy love,
And follow where thy feet have trod;
Till glorious from thy heaven above
Shall come the City of our God.

*F. M. North**

144

St. Andrew 87.87.

JESUS, by thy simple beauty,
By thy depth of love unknown,
We are drawn to earnest duty,
We come near the Father's throne.

When we read the sacred pages
Of that life so pure and true,
Stars of hope across the ages
Rise in glory on our view.

Faith and hope and love shine o'er us,
Make our daily lives divine;
Friend and Brother gone before us,
Be our thoughts and deeds like thine.

Praise to thee, our heavenly Father,
That when human eyes grow dim,
And when shadows darkly gather,
Shines a holy light through him.

*Anon.**

PALM SUNDAY AND PASSIONTIDE

145

Winchester New L.M.

RIDE on! ride on in majesty!
Hark! all the tribes Hosanna cry!
Thy humble beast pursues his road,
With palms and scattered garments strowed.

Ride on! ride on in majesty!
In lowly pomp ride on to die!
O Christ, thy triumphs now begin
O'er captive death and conquered sin.

Ride on! ride on in majesty!
The wingèd squadrons of the sky
Look down with sad and wondering eyes
To see the approaching sacrifice.

Ride on! ride on in majesty!
Thy last and fiercest strife is nigh;
Bow thy meek head to mortal pain,
Then take, O Christ, thy power, and reign!

*H. H. Milman**

146

St. Theodulph 76.76.D.(with refrain)

ALL glory, laud, and honour
To thee, Messiah, King,
To whom the lips of children
Made sweet hosannas ring!
Thou art the King of Israel,
Thou David's royal Son,
Who in the Lord's name comest,
The King and Blessèd One.

The company of angels
Are praising thee on high,
And mortal men and all things
Created make reply.
The people of the Hebrews
With palms before thee went;
Our praise and prayer and anthems
Before thee we present.

To thee before thy Passion
They sang their hymns of praise;
To thee now high exalted
Our melody we raise.

Thou didst accept their praises:
  Accept the prayers we bring,
Who in all good delightest,
  Thou good and gracious King.

All glory, laud, and honour
  To thee, Messiah, King,
To whom the lips of children
  Made sweet hosannas ring!

*Theodulph of Orleans, trans. J. M. Neale**

147

St. Theodulph 76.76.D.

HOSANNA in the highest!
  Our eager hearts acclaim
The prophet of the Kingdom,
  Who bears Messiah's name.

O bold, O foolish peasants,
  To deem that he should reign!
The temple and the palace
  Look down in high disdain.

Jerusalem lies fallen,
  And pilgrims wail her pride.
The golden words of Jesus
  Have travelled far and wide.

Long ages dim the message
  And custom has sufficed
For merchants and for princes
  To bow, and own him Christ.

But when a kindred spirit
  Arises from the plain,
The men of power tremble
  And crucify again.

O first of many prophets
  Who come of simple folk
To free us from our bondage,
  To break oppression's yoke,

Restore our eyes from blindness,
Make clear the life, the way
That leads through love and justice
Unto the peace-crowned day!

*J. H. Lathrop**

148

Morning Light 76.76.D.

FROM Bethany, the Master
Comes down Mount Olive's slope;
And all the world is singing
A glad new song of hope;
Cry out, O stately cedars,
Along the rugged way!
Ye vineyards, shout Hosannas,
To greet this happy day!

The King of Love, in triumph,
Rides through the city's gate;
Rejected, scorned, yet victor –
The conqueror of hate;
O wave your green palm branches!
Extol his matchless worth!
This lowly King shall conquer
The nations of the earth.

Not of this world his kingdom –
His power is from above;
His realm is of the spirit;
His sceptre–truth and love.
He calls us to his service,
His banner is unfurled;
With thee we march, O Master,
To overcome the world.

M. F. Ham

149

Dalehurst C.M.

"REMEMBER me," the Master said,
On that forsaken night,
When from his side the nearest fled,
And death was close in sight.

Through all the following ages' track,
The world remembers yet;
With love and worship gazes back
And never can forget.

But none of us has seen his face,
Or heard the words he said;
And none can now his looks retrace
In breaking of the bread.

Oh, blest are they who have not seen,
And yet believe him still!
Who call him Lord, and vow and mean
To do his Father's will.

We hear his word along our way;
We see his light above;
"Remember" when we strive and pray,
"Remember" when we love.

N. L. Frothingham

150

Hollingside 77.77.D.

WHEN the Paschal evening fell
Deep on Kedron's hallowed dell,
When around the festal board
Sat the Apostles with their Lord,
Then his parting word he said,
Blessed the cup and brake the bread –
"This whene'er ye do or see,
Evermore remember me."

Years have passed; in every clime,
Changing with the changing time,
Varying through a thousand forms,
Torn by factions, rocked by storms,
Still the sacred table spread,
Flowing cup and broken bread,
With that parting word agree,
"Drink and eat; remember me."

When in this thanksgiving feast
We would give to God our best,
From the treasures of his might
Seeking life and love and light;
Then, O Friend of human-kind,
Make us true and firm of mind,
Pure of heart, in spirit free;
Thus may we remember thee.

A. P. Stanley

151

St. Hugh (Hopkins) C.M.

O GOD unseen, but ever near,
Our blessèd rest art thou;
And we, in love that hath no fear,
Take refuge with thee now.

All soiled with dust our pilgrim feet,
And weary with the way,
We seek thy shelter from the heat
And burden of life's day.

Oh, welcome in the wilderness
The shadow of thy love,
The stream that springs our thirst to bless,
The manna from above!

Awhile beside the fount we stay
And eat this bread of thine,
Then go rejoicing on our way,
Renewed with strength divine.

S. Longfellow, after E. Osler

152

Farrant C.M.

BENEATH the shadow of the cross,
As earthly hopes remove,
His new commandment Jesus gives,
His blessèd word of love.

O bond of union, strong and deep!
O bond of perfect peace!
Not e'en the lifted cross can harm,
If we but hold to this.

Then, Jesus, be thy spirit ours;
And swift our feet shall move
To deeds of pure self-sacrifice,
And patient tasks of love.

*S. Longfellow**

153

Redhead 77.77.

WHEN my love to God grows weak,
When for deeper faith I seek,
Then in thought I go to thee,
Garden of Gethsemane!

There I walk amid the shades,
While the lingering twilight fades,
See that suffering, friendless One
Weeping, praying there alone.

When my love for all grows weak,
When for stronger faith I seek,
Hill of Calvary! I go
To thy scenes of fear and woe –

There behold his agony
Suffered on the bitter tree,
See his anguish, see his faith,
Love triumphant still in death.

Then to life I turn again,
Learning all the worth of pain,
Learning all the might that lies
In a full self-sacrifice.

*J. R. Wreford, altered S. Longfellow**

154

St. Cross *L.M.*

A VOICE upon the midnight air,
Where Kedron's moonlit waters stray,
Weeps forth, in agony of prayer,
"O Father! take this cup away!"

Ah! Thou who sorrowest unto death,
We conquer in thy mortal fray;
And Earth, for all her children, saith,
"O God! take not this cup away!"

O Lord of sorrow, meekly die:
Thou'lt heal or hallow all our woe;
Thy name refresh the mourner's sigh,
Thy peace revive the faint and low.

Great Chief of faithful souls, arise!
None else can lead the martyr-band,
Who teach the brave how peril flies,
When faith, unarmed, uplifts the hand.

O King of earth, the cross ascend!
O'er climes and ages 'tis thy throne;
Where'er thy fading eye may bend,
The desert blooms, and is thine own.

Thy parting blessing, Lord, we pray;
Make but one fold below, above;
And when we go the last lone way,
O give the welcome of thy love.

James Martineau

155

Passion Chorale *76.76.D.*

THE sacred Cross of Jesus
Stands like a beacon light,
To guide the storm-tossed wanderer
Across the gloom of night.
Amidst the crash of tempests
It stands for ever sure;
Upon the Rock of Ages
It shall for aye endure.

Beneath the Cross of Jesus
  I rest my weary soul,
When life is dark and troubled,
  And floods of sorrow roll.
Upon his love I ponder,
  That led him there to die,
Till all my troubles vanish,
  And heaven seems very nigh.

O blessèd Cross of Jesus,
  O wondrous throne of grace,
On thee, in glory shining,
  The light of heaven we trace!
On thee, for aye uplifted,
  In radiance from above,
Shines down the weary ages
  The mystery of Love!

H. W. Hawkes

156

Passion Chorale 76.76.D.

O SACRED Head, sore wounded,
  With grief and pain weighed down,
How scornfully surrounded
  With thorns, thine only crown!
How pale art thou with anguish,
  With sore abuse and scorn!
How does that visage languish
  Which once was bright as morn!

O Lord of life and glory,
  What bliss till now was thine!
I read the wondrous story,
  I joy to call thee mine.
Thy grief and thy compassion
  Were all for sinners' gain;
Mine, mine was the transgression,
  But thine the deadly pain.

What language shall I borrow
  To praise thee, dearest friend,
For this thy dying sorrow,
  Thy pity without end?
Lord, make me thine for ever,
  Nor let me faithless prove;
O let me never, never
  Abuse such dying love!

Be near me, Lord, when dying;
  O show thy cross to me,
That I, for succour flying,
  My eyes may fix on thee;
And then, thy grace receiving,
  Let faith my fears dispel,
For whoso dies believing
  In thee, dear Lord, dies well.

Paul Gerhardt
trans. James Waddell Alexander and
Rupert E. Davies

157

Cross of Jesus 87.87.

IN the Cross of Christ I glory,
  Towering o'er the wrecks of time;
All the light of sacred story
  Gathers round its head sublime.

When the woes of life o'ertake me,
  Hopes deceive, and fears annoy,
Never shall the Cross forsake me:
  Lo, it glows with peace and joy.

When the sun of bliss is beaming
  Light and love upon my way,
From the Cross the radiance streaming
  Adds more lustre to the day.

Bane and blessing, pain and pleasure,
By the Cross are sanctified;
Peace is there, that knows no measure,
Joys that through all time abide.

In the Cross of Christ I glory,
Towering o'er the wrecks of time;
All the light of sacred story
Gathers round its head sublime.

Sir John Bowring

158

Rockingham L.M.

WHEN I survey the wondrous cross,
On which the Prince of Glory died,
My richest gain I count but loss,
And pour contempt on all my pride.

See from his head, his hands, his feet,
Sorrow and love flow mingled down;
Did e'er such love and sorrow meet,
Or thorns compose so rich a crown?

His dying crimson, like a robe,
Spreads o'er his body on the tree;
Then am I dead to all the globe,
And all the globe is dead to me.

Were the whole realm of nature mine,
That were a present far too small;
Love so amazing, so divine,
Demands my soul, my life, my all.

Isaac Watts

159

Veni Emmanuel 10 10.10 10.10 10.

O COME, Creator Spirit, with thy breath
Dispel the slothful ease that yields to death;
Reveal thy truth where mists have veiled our sight;
Renew our ancient courage for the fight.
Rejoice! Rejoice! A Knight of Nazareth
Rode forth alone to triumph over death.

What noble hosts have followed in his wake
To fight the endless battle for his sake:
They bore his banner high amid the throng,
And all their valour lives in book and song.
  Rejoice! Rejoice! The Knight of Nazareth
  Rode forth with these to triumph over death.

But souls unresting thread the sunless maze
Of city toil, and see not through the haze
What weapons of the Spirit we may wield –
What banners go before us in the field.
  Rejoice! Rejoice! The Knight of Nazareth
  Shall lead them forth to triumph over death.

Thou happy soul, to whom a sacred sword
And armour were a birthright from thy Lord,
Go arm the feeble fighter in the dust;
So shall thine own bright weapons never rust.
  Rejoice! Rejoice! The Knight of Nazareth
  Rides forth with thee to triumph over death.

O Come, Creator Spirit, let thy breath
Bring valour to each soul who travaileth
To make in toiling town and mine and mill
The earth a shining mirror of thy will.
  Rejoice! Rejoice! The Knight of Nazareth
  Shall lead the world to triumph over death.

*R. P. Howgrave-Graham**

EASTER

160 *Easter Hymn 77.77. with Alleluias*

JESUS Christ is risen today, *Alleluia!*
Our triumphant holy day. *Alleluia!*
Lately on the Cross undone, *Alleluia!*
Now his victory is won. *Alleluia!*

Hymns of joy then let us sing,
Unto God, our heavenly King.
Death is slain since Christ is raised,
God the Conqueror be praised.

We shall follow where our Lord,
To the Father's throne has soared;
And above the heavens sing
Alleluia to our King.

Adapted from Lyra Davidica, 1708

161

Easter Hymn 77.77. *with Alleluias*

THOU whose love has given us birth, *Alleluia!*
Pilgrims on the fruitful earth, *Alleluia!*
Evermore our souls defend, *Alleluia!*
Steadfast, trusting, to the end. *Alleluia!*

They whose life is hid in God,
Shepherded with staff and rod,
Singing in the shadowed vale,
Know that death shall not prevail.

Hearts are strong, and voices sing
Where, O death, is now thy sting?
When God taketh what he gave
Where thy victory, O grave?

His the love that shall endure,
Ours to trust that promise sure;
Death's dominion now is past,
In God's love we rest at last!

H. W. Foote

162

Irby 87.87.77.

EASTER flowers, Easter carols,
Deck the altar, fill the air;
Glorious dawns the happy morning
O'er a world so bright and fair.
Alleluia, let us sing,
Alleluia to our King!

Now the clouds of night are broken,
 Doubt and darkness flee away,
And on this bright Easter morning
 Sing we now the triumph lay.

Past is all the gloom and sadness,
 Easter joys around us shine,
Turned is sorrow into gladness,
 Death is changed to life divine.

Purer lives and joyful music
 Help us, Lord, to bring to thee,
Till we join the choir immortal
 Who from sin and death are free
 Alleluia, still to sing,
 Alleluia to our King!

Anon.

163

Victory 888. with Alleluias

PAST are the cross, the scourge, the thorn,
The scoffing tongue, the gibe, the scorn,
And brightly breaks the Easter morn.
Alleluia!

Gone are the gloomy clouds of night;
The shades of death are put to flight:
And from the tomb beams heavenly light.

And so, in sorrow dark and drear,
Though black the night, the morn is near;
Soon shall the heavenly day appear.

And when death's darkness dims our eyes,
From out the gloom our souls shall rise
In deathless glory to the skies.

Then let us raise the glorious strain,
Love's triumph over sin and pain,
Faith's victory over terror's reign!

A. C. Jewitt

164

Morning Light 76.76.D.

THE Light along the ages
  Shines brighter as it goes;
From age to age more glorious
  Its radiant splendour grows.
Our life, begun so lowly,
  Now soars to heaven above,
To share, in life eternal,
  The joys of endless love!

We thank thee, O our Father,
  For every gift of thine;
All speak alike the bounty
  Of tenderness divine;
But, every gift surpassing,
  This wondrous thought we own –
The Son of Man is risen
  To dwell before thy throne!

Wherever goodness reigneth
  The soul of Christ lives on,
And every Christlike spirit
  Shall rise where he hath gone:
Earth's dust hath served its mission;
  Henceforth the soul is free,
And through the heights of being
  Ascends, O God, to thee!

W. G. Tarrant

165

Tottenham C.M.

JESUS has lived, and we would bring
  The world's glad thanks to-day,
And at his feet, while anthems ring,
  A grateful offering lay.

Jesus has died; but his pure life,
  So perfect and sublime,
Remains to conquer sin and strife
  In every age and clime.

Jesus yet lives – above, below,
  Triumphant over death;
And in his name we face each foe,
  And win the fight of faith.

Jesus yet lives; and oh, may we,
  While in this valley dim,
So feel our glorious destiny
  That we may live like him!

W. R. Alger

166

Stuttgart 87.87.

JESUS died, but Christ has triumphed.
  Broken now the chains of death:
From the tomb comes God's anointed,
  Kindling cold hearts with his breath.

Now at last we see his purpose,
  Breaking through like sunburst bright:
Liberation for God's people
  Ends humanity's long night.

For there is a Spirit greater,
  Who has now the victory;
And our God indwells the human,
  Striving for our liberty.

And that Spirit dwelt in Jesus,
  Teaching us that love redeems;
How God, through a man's compassion,
  Gains great ends by human means.

But for love and life undying
  Death of self must be the key;
Jesus died to bear this witness
  And Christ rose to make us free.

Clifford Martin Reed

167

Llanfair 77.77.with Alleluias

LO, the earth is risen again, *Alleluia!*
From the winter's bond and pain! *Alleluia!*
Bring we leaf and flower and spray, *Alleluia!*
To adorn this holy day. *Alleluia!*

Once again the word comes true,
Lo, he maketh all things new!
Now the dark, cold days are o'er,
Light and gladness are before.

How our hearts leap with the spring!
How our spirits soar and sing!
Light is victor over gloom,
Life triumphant o'er the tomb.

Change then, mourning into praise,
And, for dirges, anthems raise:
All our fears and griefs shall be
Lost in immortality.

S. Longfellow

168

Noel Nouvelet 1111.1011.

NOW the green blade rises from the buried grain,
Wheat that in the dark earth many days has lain;
Love lives again, that with the dead has been:

Love is come again, like wheat that springs up green.

In the grave they laid him, Love whom men had slain,
Thinking that he never would awake again,
Laid in the earth like grain that sleeps unseen:

Forth he came at Easter, like the risen grain,
He that for the three days in the grave had lain,
Quick from the dead my risen Lord is seen:

When our hearts are wintry, grieving, or in pain,
Then your touch can call us back to life again,
Fields of our hearts that dead and bare have been:

*J. M. C. Crum**

169

Ellacombe C.M.D.

THE day of resurrection,
Earth, tell it out abroad!
The passover of gladness,
The passover of God!
From death to life eternal,
From earth unto the sky,
Our Christ has brought us over
With hymns of victory.

Our hearts be pure from evil,
That we may see aright
The Lord in rays eternal
Of resurrection light;
And, listening to his accents,
May hear, so calm and plain,
His own 'All hail!' and, hearing,
May raise the victor strain.

Now let the heavens be joyful,
Let earth her song begin,
The round world keep high triumph,
And all that is therein;
Let all things seen and unseen
Their notes of gladness blend,
For Christ the Lord is risen,
Our joy that has no end.

John of Damascus trans. J. M. Neale

THE GIFT OF THE SPIRIT

170

St. Cuthbert 86.84.

OUR Lord and Master, ere he breathed
His tender, last farewell,
A Guide, a Comforter bequeathed,
With us to dwell.

He came in tongues of living flame,
To teach, convince, subdue;
All-powerful as the wind he came,
As viewless too.

He comes his influence to impart,
A gracious, willing guest,
While he can find one humble heart
Wherein to rest.

And his that gentle voice we hear,
Soft as the breath of even,
That checks each fault, that calms each fear,
And speaks of heaven.

And every virtue we possess,
And every victory won,
And every thought of holiness,
Are his alone.

Spirit of purity and grace,
Our weakness, pitying, see;
O make our hearts thy dwelling-place,
And worthier thee.

*Henriette Auber**

171

Herongate L.M.

CREATOR Spirit, grant us grace
To make our hearts thy dwelling-place;
Drive far away each thought of sin,
Shed thy bright beams on all within.

Pour down thine unction from above,
Thou Lord of purity and love;
Cleanse thou the inward eye, that we
The eternal light unveiled may see.

Through thee the waters teeming roll,
Thy breath gives us a living soul;
Through thee the tongues of humankind
Their unity of utterance find.

Without thee all our prayers are vain;
Thou only canst our souls sustain;
Through every age thy saints confess
Thy power to purify and bless.

So, Lord, thy Pentecostal grace
Give now in this thy dwelling-place;
Make darkness light, and false thoughts true;
Yea, in our souls make all things new.

*Sarum Missal, trans. E. P. Plumptre**

172

Veni Creator L.M.

SPIRIT of God, our souls inspire,
And lighten with celestial fire;
Thou the anointing Spirit art,
Who dost thy sevenfold gifts impart:

Thy blessed unction from above
Is comfort, life, and fire of love;
Enable with perpetual light
The dullness of our blinded sight:

Anoint and cheer our soilèd face
With the abundance of thy grace;
Keep far our foes, give peace at home;
Where thou art guide no ill can come.

Teach us to know thee, Gracious One,
As Holy Spirit, Father, Son;
That through the ages all along
This may be our endless song:

"Praise to thy eternal merit,
Sovereign and life-giving Spirit. Amen."

9th Century
trans. John Cosin, altered T. Cross

173

Moscow 664.6664.

THOU, whose almighty word
Chaos and darkness heard,
And took their flight,
Hear us, we humbly pray;
And where the gospel's day
Sheds not its glorious ray,
Let there be light!

Thou who didst come to bring
On thy redeeming wing
Healing and sight,
Health to the sick in mind,
Sight to the inly blind,
O now for humankind
Let there be light!

Spirit of truth and love,
Life-giving, holy dove,
Speed forth thy flight;
Move on the waters' face,
Bearing the lamp of grace,
And in earth's darkest place
Let there be light!

*J. Marriott**

174

Glenfinlas 65.65.

HOLY Spirit, hear us;
Help us while we sing;
Breath into the music
Of the praise we bring.

Holy Spirit, prompt us
When we kneel to pray;
Nearer come, and teach us
What we ought to say.

Holy Spirit, shine thou
On the book we read;
Gild its holy pages
With the light we need.

Holy Spirit, give us
Each a lowly mind,
Make us more like Jesus,
Gentle, pure, and kind.

Holy Spirit, help us
Daily by thy might,
What is wrong to conquer,
And to choose the right.

W. H. Parker

175

Richmond C.M.

SPIRIT divine! attend our prayer,
And make our hearts thy home;
Descend with all thy gracious power;
Come, Holy Spirit, come!

Come as the light; to waiting minds
That long the truth to know,
Reveal the narrow path of right,
The way of duty show.

Come as the fire; enkindle now
The sacrificial flame,
Till our whole souls an offering be
In love's redeeming name.

Come as the dew; on hearts that pine
Descend in this still hour,
Till every barren place shall own
With joy thy quickening power.

Come as the wind; sweep clean away
What dead within us lies,
And search and freshen all our souls
With living energies.

A. Reed, altered S. Longfellow

176

Lauds 77.77.

THERE'S a spirit in the air,
Telling Christians everywhere:
Praise the love that Christ revealed,
Living, working, in our world.

Lose your shyness, find your tongue;
Tell the world what God has done:
God in Christ has come to stay;
Live tomorrow's life today!

When believers break the bread,
When a hungry child is fed,
Praise the love that Christ revealed,
Living, working, in our world.

Still the Spirit gives us light,
Seeing wrong and setting right:
God in Christ has come to stay;
Live tomorrow's life today!

When a stranger's not alone,
Where the homeless find a home,
Praise the love that Christ revealed,
Living, working, in our world.

May the Spirit fill our praise,
Guide our thoughts and change our ways:
God in Christ has come to stay;
Live tomorrow's life today!

There's a Spirit in the air,
Calling people everywhere:
Praise the love that Christ revealed,
Living, working, in our world.

Brian A. Wren

177

Carlisle S.M.

BREATHE on me, Breath of God,
Fill me with life anew,
That I may love what thou dost love,
And do what thou wouldst do.

Breath on me, Breath of God,
Until my heart is pure,
Until with thee I will one will,
To do or to endure.

Breathe on me, Breath of God,
Till I am wholly thine,
Till all this earthly part of me
Glows with thy fire divine.

Breathe on me, Breath of God,
So shall I never die,
But live with thee the perfect life
Of thine eternity.

E. Hatch

178

Spirit of the living God Irregular

SPIRIT of the living God,
Fall afresh on me.
Spirit of the living God,
Fall afresh on me.
Break me, melt me,
Mould me, fill me.
Spirit of the living God,
Fall afresh on me.

Daniel Iverson

179

Charity 777.5.

MIGHTY Spirit, gracious Guide,
Let thy light in us abide;
Light supreme o'er all beside –
  Holy, heavenly love.

Faith that mountains could remove,
Tongues of earth and heaven above,
Knowledge – all things – empty prove,
  Without heavenly love.

Though I as a martyr bleed,
Give my goods the poor to feed,
All is vain if love I need;
  Therefore, give me love.

Love is kind, and suffers long;
Love is meek, and thinks no wrong;
Love than death itself more strong;
  Therefore give us love.

Prophecy will fade away,
Melting in the light of day;
Love will ever with us stay;
  Therefore give us love.

Faith will vanish into sight,
Hope be emptied in delight;
Love in heaven will shine more bright;
  Therefore give us love.

Faith and hope and love we see
Joining hand in hand agree:
But the greatest of the three,
  And the best, is love.

*C. Wordsworth**

180

Abends L.M.

SPIRIT of Truth! who makest bright
All souls that long for heavenly light,
Appear, and on my darkness shine;
Descend, and be my guide divine.

Spirit of Power! whose might doth dwell
Full in the souls thou lovest well,
Unto this fainting heart draw near,
And be my daily quickener.

Spirit of Joy! who makest glad
Each broken heart by sin made sad,
Pour on this mourning soul thy cheer;
Give me to bless my comforter.

O tender Spirit! who dost mourn
Whene'er from thee thy people turn,
Give me each day to grieve thee less,
Enjoy my fuller faithfulness:

Till thou shalt make me meet to bear
The blessing of heaven's holy air,
The light wherein no darkness is,
The eternal, overflowing bliss.

*T. H. Gill**

181

Buckland 77.77.

HOLY Spirit, Truth divine,
Dawn upon this soul of mine!
Word of God and inward Light,
Wake my spirit, clear my sight.

Holy Spirit, Love divine,
Glow within this heart of mine!
Kindle every high desire,
Perish self in thy pure fire!

Holy Spirit, Power divine,
Fill and nerve this will of mine!
By thee may I strongly live,
Bravely bear and nobly strive.

Holy Spirit, Right divine,
King within my conscience reign!
Be my law and I shall be
Firmly bound, for ever free.

Holy Spirit, Peace divine,
Still this restless heart of mine!
Speak to calm this tossing sea,
Stayed in thy tranquillity.

Holy Spirit, Joy divine,
Gladden thou this heart of mine!
In the desert ways I sing –
"Spring, O Well, for ever spring!"

S. Longfellow

182

Dix 77.77.77.

GRACIOUS Spirit, dwell with me;
I myself would gracious be,
And, with words that help and heal,
Would thy life in mine reveal;
And with actions bold and meek
Christ's own gracious spirit speak.

Truthful Spirit, dwell with me;
I myself would truthful be,
And with wisdom kind and clear
Let thy life in mine appear;
And with actions neighbourly
Follow Christ's sincerity.

Tender Spirit, dwell with me;
I myself would tender be;
Shut my heart up like a flower
At temptation's testing hour;
Open it when shines the sun,
And thy love by fragrance own.

Silent Spirit, dwell with me;
I myself would quiet be,
Quiet as the growing blade
Which through earth its way has made;
Silently, like morning light,
Putting mists and chills to flight.

Mighty Spirit, dwell with me;
I myself would mighty be,
Mighty so as to prevail
Where unaided I must fail;
Ever by a mighty hope
Pressing on and bearing up.

Holy Spirit, dwell with me;
I myself would holy be;
Separate from sin, I would
Choose and cherish all things good;
And whatever I can be
I would consecrate to thee.

*T. T. Lynch**

CHRISTIAN DISCIPLESHIP

183

St. Valentine *L.M.D.*

O MASTER, let me walk with thee
In lowly paths of service free:
Tell me thy secret; help me bear
The strain of toil, the fret of care;
Help me the slow of heart to move
By some clear winning word of love;
Teach me the wayward feet to stay,
And guide them in the homeward way.

Teach me thy patience; still with thee
In closer, dearer company,
In work that keeps faith firm and strong,
In trust that triumphs over wrong,
In hope that sends a shining ray
Far down the future's broadening way;
In peace that only thou canst give,
With thee, O Master, let me live!

*W. Gladden**

184

Buckland 77.77.

GOD of Jesus, hear me now
Take the true disciple's vow;
Thou so good, so just, so kind,
Fill me with his holy mind.

Plant, and root, and fix in me
Trust, as of a child, in thee;
Settled peace I then shall find;
Give me, Lord, his quiet mind.

I shall suffer and fulfil
All my Father's gracious will,
Be in all alike resigned;
Give me, Lord, his patient mind.

When his faith is rooted here,
Perfect love shall cast out fear;
Fear doth servile spirits bind;
Give me, Lord, his noble mind.

Lowly, loving, just, and pure,
May I to the end endure,
Be no more to ill inclined!
Give me, Lord, his constant mind.

*Charles Wesley**

185

St. Bride S.M.

A VOICE by Jordan's shore,
A summons stern and clear:
Reform, be just, and sin no more!
God's judgement draweth near!

A voice by Galilee,
A holier voice I hear:
Love God, thy neighbour love, for see,
God's mercy draweth near!

O voice of Duty, still
Speak forth: I hear with awe;
In thee I own the sovereign will,
Obey the sovereign law.

Thou higher voice of Love,
Yet speak thy word in me;
Through Duty, let me upward move
To thy pure liberty!

S. Longfellow

186

Cheltenham 76.76.D.

MY Master was a worker,
With daily work to do,
And one who would be like him
Must be a worker too;
Then welcome honest labour,
And honest labour's fare,
For where there is a worker
His follower is there.

My Master was a neighbour
A faithful friend and true,
And one who would be like him
Must be a neighbour too;
In happy hours of singing,
In silent hours of care,
Where goes a caring neighbour
His follower is there.

My Master was a helper,
  The woes of life he knew,
And one who would be like him
  Must be a helper too;
The burden will grow lighter
  If each will take a share,
And where there is a helper
  His follower is there.

My brothers, then, and sisters
  Together let us be,
For he who is our Master,
  Taught us humanity.
And those who would be like him
  Are wanted everywhere,
For where they love each other
  His followers are there.

*W. G. Tarrant**
altered T.Cross

187

Kingsfold C.M.D.

AMID the din of earthly strife,
  Amid the busy crowd,
The whispers of eternal life
  Are lost in clamours loud;
When, lo! I find a healing balm;
  The world grows dim to me;
My spirit rests in sudden calm
  With Christ in Galilee!

I linger near him in the throng,
  And listen to his voice;
I feel my weary soul grow strong,
  My saddened heart rejoice.
Amid the storms that darkly frown
  I hear him speak within,
And lay my heavy burden down
  Relieved of every sin.

My vision swiftly fades away,
The world is round me still;
But Jesus seems with me to stay,
His promise to fulfil.
And toil and duty easier seem
While he abides with me;
My heart is rested by my dream
Of Christ in Galilee!

*H. W. Hawkes**

188

Westminster C.M.

FORTH went the heralds of the Cross,
No dangers made them pause;
They counted all the world but loss
For their great Master's cause.

Through looks of fire and words of scorn,
Serene their path they trod;
And, to the dreary dungeon borne,
Sang praises unto God.

Friends dropped the hand they clasped before,
Love changed to cruel hate,
And home to them was home no more;
Yet mourned they not their fate.

In all his dark and dread array,
Death rose upon their sight;
But calmly still they kept their way,
And shrank not from the fight.

They knew to whom their trust was given,
They could not doubt his word;
Before them beamed the light of heaven –
The presence of their Lord.

W. Gaskell

189

Mirfield C.M.

GOD'S trumpet wakes the slumbering world:
  Now each one to his post!
The red-cross banner is unfurled;
  Who joins the glorious host?

He who, in fealty to the truth,
  And counting all the cost,
Doth consecrate his generous youth,
  He joins the noble host.

She who, no anger on her tongue,
  Nor any idle boast,
Bears steadfast witness against wrong,
  She joins the sacred host.

Those who, with calm, undaunted will,
  Ne'er count the battle lost,
But, though defeated, battle still,
  They join the faithful host.

Those who are ready for the cross,
  The cause despised love most,
And shun not pain or shame or loss,
  They join the martyr host.

*S. Longfellow**

190

Intercessor 11 10.11 10.

HE whom the Master loved has truly spoken:
  The holier worship, which God deigns to bless,
Restores the lost, binds up the spirit broken,
  And feeds the widow and the fatherless.

O loving soul, fold to thy heart thy neighbour;
  Where pity dwells the peace of God is there;
To worship rightly is to love each other;
  Each smile a hymn, each kindly deed a prayer.

Follow with reverent steps the great example
  Of him whose holy work was doing good:
So shall the wide earth seem our Father's temple,
  Each loving life a psalm of gratitude.

Then shall all shackles fall; the stormy clangour
  Of wild war-music o'er the earth shall cease;
Love shall tread out the baleful fire of anger,
  And in its ashes plant the tree of peace.

*J. G. Whittier**

191

St. Peter C.M.

THOUGH lowly here our lot may be,
  High work have we to do,
In faith and trust to follow him
  Whose lot was lowly too.

Our days of darkness we may bear,
  Strong in a Father's love,
Leaning on his almighty arm,
  And fixed our hopes above.

Our lives, enriched with gentle thoughts
  And loving deeds, may be
A stream that still the nobler grows,
  The nearer to the sea.

To duty firm, to conscience true,
  However tried and pressed,
In God's clear sight high work we do,
  If we but do our best.

Thus may we make the lowliest lot
  With rays of glory bright;
Thus may we turn a crown of thorns
  Into a crown of light.

W. Gaskell

192

St. Andrew 87.87.

JESUS calls us; o'er the tumult
Of our life's wild restless sea,
Day by day his clear voice soundeth,
Saying, "Christian, follow me."

As of old disciples heard it
By the Galilean lake,
Turn'd from home, and toil, and kindred,
Leaving all for his dear sake.

Jesus calls us from the worship
Of the vain world's golden store,
From each idol that would keep us,
Saying, "Christian, love me more."

In our joys and in our sorrows,
Days of toil and hours of ease,
Still he calls, in cares and pleasures,
"Christian, love me more than these."

Jesus calls us! As disciples,
Master, may we hear thy call,
Give our hearts to thy obedience,
Serve and love thee best of all.

*Cecil Frances Alexander**

193

Kilmarnock C.M.

WE bear the strain of earthly care,
But bear it not alone;
Beside us walks our Brother, Christ,
And makes our task his own.

Through din of market, whirl of wheels,
And thrust of driving trade,
We follow where the Master leads,
Serene and unafraid.

The common hopes that make us brave
Were his in Galilee;
The tasks he gives are those he gave
Beside the restless sea.

Our unity still rests in him,
The Brother of us all;
And o'er the centuries still we hear
The Master's gracious call.

*O. S. Davis**

194

St. Michael S.M.

ARM, fighters for the Lord!
The battle is with wrong;
Take shield and breastplate, helm and sword,
And sing your victory song.

Stand fast for Love, your Lord,
Faith be your mighty shield,
And let the Spirit's burning sword
Flash foremost in the field.

Truth be your buckle strong;
And Hope your helmet shine
Whene'er the battle seems too long,
And wearied hearts repine.

With news of Gospel peace
Let your swift feet be shod;
Your breastplate be the Righteousness
That keeps the heart for God.

And for the weary day,
And for the lazy arm,
For wounds, defeat, distress, dismay,
Take Prayer, the heavenly charm.

"From strength to strength," your cry;
Your battlefield the world;
Strike home, and press where Christ your Lord
His banner has unfurled.

*S. A. Brooke**

195

Bethany *87.87.D.*

FRIENDS are we, whom love is leading forth from shades of starless night –
Hearts aglow, and faces sunward – children of the morning light.
Dark the way that lies behind us, rough the path our feet have trod;
But around us clouds are breaking on the breezy hills of God.

Saviour, if to us is granted sunlight over hill and vale,
If, to drink of living water from the springs that shall not fail,
Save us from the isolation of a love-forgetful creed;
Let our joy be strong for service, rich to help in word and deed.

There are human hearts in bondage, where thy Gospel may not shine,
Where the flowers of love are blasted, well nigh quenched the spark divine;
Where the folk that use thy name are waging war's unholy strife.
And the greedy ones, unheeding, crucify the Lord of Life.

O our Master, thou hast died that souls in bonds may yet be free,
Draining deep the cup of sorrow in thy dark Gethsemane;
Conquering in the might of meekness, bringing gladness out of pain,
Changing earth's low mournful music into heaven's triumphant strain.

It is they who share thy sorrow that can share thy love divine,
They who tread with thee the wine-press that can offer heavenly wine.
Mould our lives to thy obedience, let thy Cross our souls inspire,
Take us, Lord, baptize us wholly with the Spirit and with fire.

*E. Grubb**

196

St. Philip 777.

HOLY Lord, before whose eyes
Every heart discovered lies,
Known beneath its last disguise.

Thou our every deed hast seen,
Thou behold'st the gulf between
What we are and might have been.

We have wandered far astray,
We have given our wills away;
O reclaim them Lord, we pray.

Lord, the way to thee is won,
And thy will on earth is done,
In the spirit of thy Son.

His thy holiness makes known,
In his love outbreaks thine own,
In his Cross we find thy throne.

Here, O Father, grant that we
Evermore ourselves may see
Made at one in him with thee.

A. Bennett

197

Maidstone 77.77.D.

LORD, from whom all blessings flow,
Perfecting the Church below!
Steadfast may we cleave to thee;
Love the mystic union be:
Join our faithful spirits, join
Each to each, and all to thine:
Lead us through the paths of peace,
On to perfect holiness.

Move and actuate and guide;
Different gifts to each divide:
Placed according to thy will,
Let us all our work fulfil:
Never from our calling move;
Needful to each other prove;
Use the grace on each bestowed,
Tempered by the art of God!

Swiftly may we all agree,
Touched with softest sympathy:
There is neither bond nor free,
Great nor servile, Lord, in thee:
Love, like death, hath all destroyed,
Rendered all distinctions void;
Names and sects and parties fall:
Thou, O Lord, art all in all!

*Charles Wesley**

198

Duke Street L.M.

FIGHT the good fight with all thy might;
Christ is thy strength, and Christ thy right;
Lay hold on life, and it shall be
Thy joy and crown eternally.

Run the straight race through God's good grace,
Lift up thine eyes, and seek his face;
Life with its way before thee lies;
Christ is the path, and Christ the prize.

Cast care aside; upon thy guide
Lean, and his mercy will provide;
Lean, and the trusting soul shall prove
Christ is its life, and Christ its love.

Faint not nor fear, his arm is near;
He changes not, and thou art dear;
Only believe, and thou shalt see
That Christ is all in all to thee.

J. S. B. Monsell

199

Vox Dilecti C.M.D.

I HEARD the voice of Jesus say,
"Come unto me and rest;
Lay down, thou weary one, lay down
Thy head upon my breast."
I came to Jesus as I was,
Weary, and worn,and sad:
I found in him a resting-place,
And he has made me glad.

I hear the voice of Jesus say,
"Behold, I freely give
The living water; thirsty one,
Stoop down, and drink, and live."
I came to Jesus, and I drank
Of that life-giving stream;
My thirst was quench'd, my soul revived,
And now I live in him.

I heard the voice of Jesus say,
"I am this dark world's Light;
Look unto me, thy morn shall rise,
And all thy day be bright."
I look'd to Jesus, and I found
In him my Star, my Sun;
And in that Light of life I'll walk
Till travelling days are done.

H. Bonar

200

Stephanos/Bullinger 85.83.

ARE you weary, have life's burdens
Left you sore, distressed?
"Come to me," says One, "and coming,
Be at rest."

Has he marks to lead me to him,
If he is my guide?
"In his feet and hands are wound-prints,
And his side."

Is there diadem, as monarch,
That his brow adorns?
"Yes, a crown of cruel beauty –
But of thorns."

If I find him, if I follow,
What reward is here?
"Many a sorrow, many a labour,
Many a tear."

If I still hold closely to him,
What expect at last?
"Sorrow vanquished, labour ended,
Jordan past."

If I ask him to receive me,
Is it "No!" he'll say?
"Not till earth and not till heaven
Pass away!"

Finding, following, keeping, struggling,
Is he sure to bless?
Saints, apostles, prophets, martyrs,
Answer, "Yes!"

*Stephen the Sabaite, trans. J. M. Neale**
altered T. Cross

201

St.Peter C.M.

ONE holy Church of God appears
  Through every age and race,
Unwasted by the lapse of years,
  Unchanged by changing place.

From oldest time, on farthest shores,
  Beneath the pine or palm,
One unseen Presence she adores,
  With silence or with psalm.

Her priests God's faithful children are
  To serve the world raised up;
The pure in heart her baptized ones,
  Love her communion-cup.

The truth is her prophetic gift,
  The soul her sacred page;
And feet on mercy's errand swift
  Do make her pilgrimage.

O living Church, thine errand speed,
  Fulfil thy task sublime;
With bread of life earth's hunger feed;
  Redeem the evil time!

*S. Longfellow**

202

Richmond C.M.

CITY of God, how broad and far
  Outspread thy walls sublime!
The true thy chartered people are
  Of every age and clime.

One holy Church, one army strong,
  One steadfast high intent,
One working band, one harvest song,
  One King Omnipotent.

How purely hath thy speech come down
From our primeval youth!
How grandly hath thine empire grown
Of freedom, love, and truth!

How gleam thy watchfires through the night
With never-fainting ray!
How rise thy towers, serene and bright,
To meet the dawning day!

In vain the surge's angry shock,
In vain the drifting sands;
Unharmed upon the Eternal Rock
The Eternal City stands.

*S. Johnson**

203

St. Michael *S.M.*

COME, kingdom of our God,
Fair reign of light and love,
Shed peace and hope and joy abroad,
And wisdom from above.

Over our spirits first
Extend thy healing reign;
There raise and quench the sacred thirst
That never pains again.

Come, kingdom of our God,
And make the broad earth thine;
Stretch o'er her lands and isles the rod
That flowers with grace divine.

Soon may all tribes be blest
With fruit from life's glad tree;
And in its shade like kindred rest,
All as one family.

Come, kingdom of our God,
And raise thy glorious throne
In worlds by the undying trod,
Where God shall bless his own.

*J. Johns**

204

Golden Sheaves/St. Columba *87.87.D.(iambic)*

I SAW the City of the Lord,
Eternal its foundation,
On high its gleaming turrets soared,
The joy of every nation;
Four-square to all the lands it stood,
And thro' its portals wending,
The true, the brave, the wise, the good,
Flowed on, a stream unending.

There rulers came on pilgrimage
With million-handed labour,
There came the simple and the sage,
Each happy with his neighbour;
At peace within those mansions fair
They lived with one another,
And everyone was welcome there
Who dwelt in love together.

A temple of the Lord I saw,
All beautiful and holy,
Its light was love, its highest law
Compassion for the lowly;
And thence arose a mighty voice
Of countless voices blended,
The song of singers that rejoice,
Their night of sorrow ended.

I saw that city from afar,
A city of salvation,
And still it shineth like a star
To every generation;
And I, a pilgrim too, would press
Where God the host is guiding,
To reach the gates of righteousness,
A citizen abiding.

*W. G. Tarrant**

205

Old 120th *66.66.66.*

O THOU not made with hands,
Not throned above the skies,
Nor walled with shining walls,
Nor framed with stones of price,
More bright than gold or gem,
God's own Jerusalem!

Where'er the gentle heart
Finds courage from above,
Where'er the heart forsook
Warms with the breath of love,
Where faith bids fear depart,
City of God, thou art.

Thou art where'er the proud
In humbleness melts down;
Where self itself yields up;
Where martyrs win their crown;
Where faithful souls possess
Themselves in perfect peace.

Where in life's common ways
With cheerful feet we go,
Where in his steps we tread
Who trod the way of woe;
Where he is in the heart,
City of God, thou art.

Not throned above the skies,
Nor golden-walled afar,
But where Christ's two or three
In his name gathered are,
Be in the midst of them,
God's own Jerusalem!

F. T. Palgrave

206

Vienna 77.77.

FATHER, let thy kingdom come,
Let it come with living power;
Speak at length the final word,
Usher in the triumph hour.

As it came in days of old,
In the deepest hearts which then,
As thy martyrs, died for thee,
Let it come, O God, again.

Tyrant thrones and idol shrines,
Let them from their place be hurled;
Enter on thy better reign,
Wear the crown of this poor world.

Oh, what long, sad years have gone
Since thy Church was taught this prayer;
Oh, what eyes have watched and wept
For the dawning everywhere.

Break, triumphant day of God,
Break at last, our hearts to cheer;
Eager souls and holy songs
Wait to hail thy dawning here.

Empires, temples, sceptres, thrones,
May they all for God be won;
And by every living soul
Father, let thy will be done.

*J. P. Hopps**

207

Breslau L.M.

O THOU in lonely vigil led
To follow Truth's new risen star,
Ere yet her morning skies are red,
And vale and upland shadowed are,

Obey her call and take thy road,
  Obedient to the vision be:
Trust not in numbers; God is God,
  And one with him majority!

Soon pass the judgements of the hour,
  Forgotten are the scorn and blame;
The Word moves on, a gladdening power,
  And safe enshrines the prophet's fame.

Now, as of old, in lowly plight
  The Christ of larger faith is born:
The watching shepherds come by night,
  And then, the kings of earth at morn!

*F. L. Hosmer**

208

Deerhurst 87.87.D.

WE believe in human kindness
  Large amid the human race,
Turning from indifferent blindness
  To compassion's healing grace.
We believe in self-denial
  In the cause of greater joy;
In the love that lives through trial,
  Dying not, though death destroy.

We believe in dreams of duty
  Warning us to self-control,
Foregleams of the glorious beauty
  That shall yet transform the soul;
In the godlike wreck of nature
  Sin does in the sinner leave,
That we may regain the stature
  We have lost – we do believe.

We believe in love renewing
  All that sin has swept away,
Leaven-like its work pursuing
  Night by night and day by day.
In the power of its remoulding,
  In the grace of its reprieve,
In the glory of beholding
  Its perfection – we believe.

We believe in love eternal,
  Fixed in God's unchanging will,
That beneath the deep infernal
  Has a depth that's deeper still;
In its patience, its endurance,
  To forbear and to retrieve,
In the large and full assurance
  Of its triumph – we believe.

*Anon.**

209

St. Stephen C.M.

THE Lord will come, and not be slow:
  His footsteps cannot err:
Before him Righteousness shall go,
  His royal harbinger.

Truth from the earth, like to a flower,
  Shall bud and blossom fair;
And Justice, from her heavenly bower,
  Look down on mortals there.

Rise, Lord! judge thou the earth in might;
  This longing earth redress;
For thou art he who shall by right
  The nations all possess.

The nations all whom thou hast made
  Shall come, and all shall frame
To bow them low before thee, Lord,
  And glorify thy Name.

For great thou art, and wonders great
By thy strong hand are done:
Thou, in thy everlasting seat,
Remainest God alone.

*John Milton and James Martineau**

210

Irish C.M.

THY kingdom come – on bended knee
The passing ages pray;
And faithful souls have yearned to see
On earth that kingdom's day.

But the slow watches of the night
Not less to God belong,
And for the everlasting Right
The silent stars are strong.

And lo! already on the hills
The flags of dawn appear;
Obey God's call, you prophet souls,
Proclaim the day is near:

The day in whose clear-shining light
All wrong shall stand revealed,
When justice shall be throned in might,
And every hurt be healed:

When knowledge, hand in hand with peace,
Shall walk the earth abroad,
The day of perfect righteousness,
The promised day of God.

*F. L. Hosmer**

211

Rex gloriae 87.87.D.

How shall come thy kingdom holy,
  In which all the earth is blest,
That shall lift on high the lowly,
  And to weary souls give rest?
Not with trumpet call of legions
  Bursting through the upper sky,
Waking earth through all its regions
  With their heaven-descending cry.

Not with dash or sudden sally,
  Swooping down with rushing wing;
But as, creeping up a valley,
  Come the grasses in the spring;
First one blade and then another,
  Still advancing are they seen,
Rank on rank, each by its neighbour,
  Till each inch of ground is green.

Through the weary days of sowing,
  Burning sun and drenching shower,
Day by day, so slowly growing,
  Comes the waited harvest hour.
So the kingdom cometh ever,
  Though it seem so far away;
Each bright thought and true endeavour
  Hastens on the blessèd day.

*M. J. Savage**

212

Angel's Song L.M.

O spirit of the living God!
In all thy plenitude of grace,
Wherever human foot hath trod,
Descend on our benighted race.

Give tongues of fire and hearts of love
To preach the reconciling word;
Give thine anointing from above,
Whene'er the joyful sound is heard.

Be darkness at thy coming, light;
Confusion, order in thy path;
Souls without strength inspire with might;
Bid mercy triumph over wrath.

O Spirit of the Lord! prepare
All the round earth her God to meet;
Breathe thou abroad like morning air,
Till hearts of stone begin to beat.

Baptize the nations; far and nigh
The triumphs of the Cross record;
Thy Name, O Father, glorify,
Till all the earth shall call thee Lord.

*J. Montgomery**

213

Regent Square 87.87.87.

GOD of grace and God of glory,
On thy people pour thy power;
Crown thine ancient Church's story;
Bring her bud to glorious flower.
Grant us wisdom,
Grant us courage,
For the facing of this hour.

Lo! the hosts of evil round us
Scorn thy Christ, assail his ways!
Fears and doubts too long have bound us;
Free our hearts to work and praise.
Grant us wisdom,
Grant us courage,
For the living of these days.

Cure thy children's warring madness;
Bend our pride to thy control;
Shame our wanton, selfish gladness,
Rich in things and poor in soul.
Grant us wisdom,
Grant us courage,
Lest we miss thy kingdom's goal.

Save us from weak resignation
To the evils we deplore;
Let the search for thy salvation
Be our glory evermore.
Grant us wisdom,
Grant us courage,
Serving thee whom we adore.

H. E. Fosdick

214

St. Ethelwald S.M.

SEND down thy truth, O God!
Too long the shadows frown;
Too long the darkened way we've trod:
Thy truth, O Lord, send down!

Send down thy Spirit free,
Till wilderness and town
One temple for thy worship be:
Thy Spirit, O send down!

Send down thy love, thy life,
Our lesser lives to crown,
And cleanse them of their hate and strife,
Thy living love send down!

Send down thy peace, O Lord!
Earth's bitter voices drown
In one deep ocean of accord:
Thy peace, O God, send down!

E. R. Sill

215

Woodlands/Ellers 10 10.10 10.

GATHER us in, thou Love that fillest all;
Gather our rival faiths within thy fold;
Rend every temple-veil, and bid it fall,
That we may know that thou hast been of old;

Gather us in, we worship only thee;
In varied names we stretch a common hand;
In differing forms a common soul we see;
In many ships we seek one spirit-land;

Each sees one colour in thy rainbow light,
Each looks upon one tint and calls it heaven;
Thou art the fulness of our partial sight;
We are not perfect till we find the seven;

Some seek a Father in the heavens above;
Some ask a human image to adore;
Some crave a Spirit vast as life and love;
Within thy mansions we have all and more.

*G. Matheson**

216

Selborne L.M.

WHAT purpose burns within our hearts
That we together here should stand
Pledging each other mutual vows,
And ready hand to join in hand?

We see in vision fair a time
When evil shall have passed away;
And thus we dedicate our lives
To hasten on that blessed day.

To seek the truth whate'er it be,
  To follow it where'er it leads;
To turn to facts our dreams of good,
  And fill our lives with loving deeds:

For this we gather here to-day;
  To such a Church of God we bring
Our utmost love and loyalty,
  And make our souls an offering.

M. J. Savage

217

Holywell/Hyfrydol 87.87.D.

SING we of the Golden City
  Pictured in the legends old:
Everlasting light shines o'er it,
  Wondrous things of it are told.
Only righteous men and women
  Dwell within its gleaming walls;
Wrong is banished from its borders,
  Justice reigns within its halls.

We are builders of that City,
  All our joys and all our groans
Help to rear its shining ramparts;
  All our lives are building-stones.
For that City we must labour,
  For its sake bear pain and grief;
In it find the end of living,
  And the anchor of belief.

And the work that we have builded,
  Oft with bleeding hands and tears,
Oft in error, oft in anguish,
  Will not perish with our years.
It will last, and shine transfigured,
  In the final reign of Right;
It will pass into the splendours
  Of the City of the Light.

F. Adler

218

Hyfrydol/Ebenezer 87.87.D.

ONCE to every soul and nation
Comes the moment to decide,
In the strife of Truth with Falsehood,
For the good or evil side;
Some great cause, God's true Messiah,
Offers each the bloom or blight,
And the choice goes by for ever
'Twixt that darkness and that light.

Then to side with Truth is noble,
When we share her wretched crust,
Ere her cause bring fame and profit,
And 'tis prosperous to be just;
Then it is the brave one chooses,
While the coward stands aside,
Till the multitude make virtue
Of the faith they had denied.

Though the cause of evil prosper,
Yet 'tis Truth alone is strong;
Though her portion be the scaffold,
And upon the throne be Wrong;
Yet that scaffold sways the future,
And, behind the dim unknown,
Standeth God within the shadow,
Keeping watch above his own.

*J. R. Lowell**

219

Benson Irregular

GOD is working his purpose out as year succeeds to year.
God is working his purpose out and the time is drawing near;
Nearer and nearer draws the time, the time that shall surely be,
When the earth shall be filled with the glory of God as the waters cover the sea.

From utmost east to utmost west wherever foot hath trod;
By the mouth of many messengers goes forth the voice
of God,
"Give ear to me, ye continents, ye isles, give ear to me,
That the earth may be filled with the glory of God as
the waters cover the sea."

What can we do to work God's work, to prosper and
increase
The unity of humankind, the reign of the Prince of Peace?
What can we do to hasten the time, the time that shall
surely be,
When the earth shall be filled with the glory of God as
the waters cover the sea?

March we forth in the strength of God with the banner
of Christ unfurled,
That the light of the glorious Gospel of truth may shine
throughout the world;
Fight we the fight with sorrow and sin, to set their
captives free,
That the earth may be filled with the glory of God as
the waters cover the sea.

All we can do is nothing worth unless God blesses the deed;
Vainly we hope for the harvest-tide till God gives life to
the seed;
Yet nearer and nearer draws the time, the time that shall
surely be,
When the earth shall be filled with the glory of God as
the waters cover the sea.

*A. C. Ainger**

220

Vulpius 888. with Alleluia

FATHER of all! In time to be
Shall one great temple rise to thee –
Thy Church our broad humanity. *Alleluia!*

White flowers of love its walls shall climb,
Soft bells of peace shall ring its chime,
Its days shall all be holy time. *Alleluia!*

A heartening song shall then be heard,
The music of the world's accord,
Confessing Christ, the inward Word. *Alleluia!*

That song shall swell from shore to shore,
One hope, one faith, one love restore
The seamless robe that Jesus wore. *Alleluia!*

*J. G. Whittier**

221

Battle Hymn Irregular

MINE eyes have seen the glory of the coming of the Lord:
He is trampling out the vintage where the grapes of wrath are stored;
He hath loosed the fateful lightning of his terrible swift sword:
His truth is marching on.

Glory, glory, hallelujah,
Glory, glory, hallelujah,
Glory, glory, hallelujah,
His truth is marching on!

He hath sounded forth the trumpet that shall never call retreat;
He is sifting out the hearts of all before his judgement seat:
Oh, be swift, my soul, to answer him; be jubilant, my feet!
Our God is marching on.

Glory, glory, hallelujah,
Glory, glory, hallelujah,
Glory, glory, hallelujah,
Our God is marching on!

In the beauty of the lilies, Christ was born across the sea,
With a glory in his bosom that transfigures you and me:
As he died to make us holy, let us live to make all free!
While God is marching on.

Glory, glory, hallelujah,
Glory, glory, hallelujah,
Glory, glory, hallelujah,
While God is marching on.

*Julia Ward Howe**

222

Vision Irregular

FROM age to age they gather, all the brave of heart
and strong,
In the strife of truth with error, of the right against the
wrong;
I can see their gleaming banner, I can hear their triumph
song;
The truth is marching on!

For in this sign we conquer; 'tis the symbol of our faith,
Made holy by the might of love triumphant over death;
"He shall find his life who loseth it," for evermore it saith:
The right is marching on!

The earth is circling onward out of shadow into light,
The stars keep watch above our way, however dark the
night;
And for every martyr's stripe there glows a bar of
morning bright,
And love is marching on!

Lead on, O cross of martyr faith, with thee is victory;
Shine forth, O stars and reddening dawn, the full day
yet shall be;
On the earth his kingdom cometh, and with joy our
eyes shall see;
Our God is marching on.

*F. L. Hosmer**

223

Petersham C.M.D.

We limit not the truth of God
To our poor reach of mind,
By notions of our day and sect,
Crude, partial, and confined;
No, let a new and better hope
Within our hearts be stirred;
The Lord hath yet more light and truth
To break forth from his word.

Who dares to bind to his dull sense
The oracles of heaven,
For all the nations, tongues, and climes,
And all the ages given?
That universe, how much unknown!
That ocean unexplored!
The Lord hath yet more light and truth
To break forth from his word.

Darkling our faithful forebears went
The first steps of the way;
'Twas but the dawning, yet to grow
Into the perfect day,
And grow it shall; our glorious Sun
More fervid rays afford;
The Lord hath yet more light and truth
To break forth from his word.

The valleys past, ascending still,
  Our souls would higher climb,
And look down from supernal heights
  On all the bygone time.
Upward we press; the air is clear,
  And the sphere-music heard;
The Lord hath yet more light and truth
  To break forth from his word.

*G. Rawson**

224

Dominus Regit Me *87.87.(iambic)*

OUR founders' faith, we'll sing of thee,
  Dear faith, which still we cherish:
Nor may their children's children see
  That faith decay and perish.

We may not think our founders' thought;
  Their creeds our lips may alter;
But in the faith they dearly bought
  Our hearts shall never falter.

Oh, may that faith our hearts inspire
  To earnest thought and labour,
That we may share its heavenly fire
  With every friend and neighbour:

This faith in God, in humankind,
  This faith in truth and beauty,
In freedom's might, and reason's right,
  And all-controlling duty!

*W. G. Tarrant**

225

Watchman 64.64.66.64.

HIGH o'er the lonely hills
Black turns to grey,
Birdsong the valley fills,
Mists fold away;
Grey wakes to green again,
Beauty is seen again –
Gold and serene again
Dawneth the day.

So, o'er the hills of life,
Stormy, forlorn,
Out of the cloud and strife
Sunrise is born;
Swift grows the light for us;
Ended is night for us;
Soundless and bright for us
Breaketh God's morn.

Hear we no beat of drums,
Fanfare nor cry,
When Christ the herald comes
Quietly nigh;
Splendour he makes on earth;
Colour awakes on earth;
Suddenly breaks on earth
Light from the sky.

Bid then farewell to sleep;
Rise up and run!
What though the hill be steep?
Strength's in the sun.
Now shall you find at last
Night's left behind at last,
For humankind all at last
Day has begun!

*Jan Struther**

226

Samson L.M.

O SOMETIMES gleams upon our sight,
Through present wrong, the eternal Right;
And step by step, since earth was made,
Our steady gain is thus displayed;

That all of good the past hath had
Remains to make our own time glad –
Our common daily life divine,
And every land a Palestine.

For still the new transcends the old
In signs and wonders manifold;
We need but open eye and ear
To see God's mysteries always here.

Through the harsh noises of our day
A low, soft prelude finds its way;
Through clouds of doubt, and creeds of fear,
A light is breaking, calm and clear.

Henceforth my heart shall sigh no more
For olden time and holier shore:
God's love and blessing, then and there,
Are now and here, and everywhere.

*J. G. Whittier**

227

Nativity C.M.

COME, let us join with faithful souls
Our song of faith to sing;
One fellowship in heart are we,
And one our Lord and King.

Faithful are all who love the truth
And dare the truth to tell,
Who steadfast stand at God's right hand
And strive to serve him well.

And faithful are the gentle hearts
To whom the power is given
Of every hearth to make a home,
Of every home a heaven.

O mighty host! No tongue can tell
The numbers of its throng;
No words can sound the music vast
Of its grand battle-song.

From step to step it wins its way
Against a world of sin;
Part of the battle-field is won,
And part is yet to win.

O Lord of Hosts, our faith renew,
And grant us, in thy love,
To sing the songs of victory
With faithful souls above.

*W. G. Tarrant**

228

Venice S.M.

RISE up, and heed God's call!
Have done with lesser things;
Give heart and soul and mind and strength
To serve the King of kings.

Rise up, and heed God's call!
His kingdom tarries long;
Bring in the day of fellowship
And end the night of wrong.

Rise up, and heed God's call!
The Church for you doth wait;
Her strength unequal to her task;
Rise up and make her great!

Lift high the Cross of Christ!
Tread where his feet have trod;
And following the Son of Man
Come heed the call of God!

*William Pierson Merrill**

Reprinted by permission of the editor, The Presbyterian Outlook, Richmond Va.

229

St. Mary C.M.

THOU long disowned, reviled, oppressed,
Strange friend of human kind,
Seeking through weary years a rest
Within our hearts to find;

How late thy bright, majestic brow
Breaks through these clouds of sin!
Hail, Truth divine! we know thee now;
Angel of God, come in!

Come, though with purifying fire
And desolating sword,
Thou of all nations the desire,
Earth waits thy cleansing word.

Struck by the lightning of thy glance
Let old oppressions die!
Before thy cloudless countenance
Let fear and falsehood fly!

Anoint our eyes with healing grace,
To see, as not before,
Our Father in our neighbour's face,
Our Maker in his poor.

Flood our dark life with golden day:
Convince, subdue, enthral;
Then to a mightier yield thy sway
And Love be all in all.

*Eliza Scudder**

230

Mountain Christian *76.76. D. Irregular*

FOR the might of thine arm we bless thee, our God,
our founders' God;
Thou hast kept thy pilgrim people by the strength of
thy staff and rod;
Thou hast called us to the journey which faithless feet
ne'er trod;
For the might of thine arm we bless thee, our God, our
founders' God.

For the love of Christ constraining that bound their
hearts as one;
For the faith in truth and freedom in which their work
was done;
For the peace of God's evangel wherewith their feet
were shod;
For the might of thine arm we bless thee, our God, our
founders' God.

We are watchers of a beacon whose light must never
die;
We are guardians of an altar that shows thee ever nigh;
We are children of thy faithful who sleep beneath the
sod;
For the might of thine arm we bless thee, our God, our
founders' God.

May the shadow of thy presence around our camp be
spread;
Baptize us with the courage with which thou blessed
our dead;
O keep us in the pathway their saintly feet have trod;
For the might of thine arm we bless thee, our God, our
founders' God.

*C. S. Horne**

231

Melita 88.88.88.

O GOD who at creation's birth
  Dispelled the darkness from the deep;
Whose Spirit bade the new formed earth
  Awaken from her primal sleep;
We thank thee for thy growing light
To guide the people's steps aright.

O Truth whose flame the prophets led,
  Whose splendour shames our base desires,
Thy holiest ray in Jesus shed,
  Our souls to worthier quest inspires;
Then grant us growing light, that we
More perfectly thy glory see.

From thee, O Light of life and love,
  All beauty and all virtue shine;
Illuminate us from above
  Until our spirit mirrors thine;
And while we strive thy will to know,
Let faith increase and vision grow.

Not for ourselves alone we pray
  Thy growing light, thy Spirit's fire;
But for all pilgrims on life's way
  Who seek thy truth with strong desire;
That they, with us, may see thy face,
And know the fulness of thy grace.

Then shall this world, so marred by wrong,
  Each blackened city, crowded street,
All peoples who for freedom long,
  Thy kingdom's dawn arise to greet:
And in thy light, renewed in mind
Thy liberty and peace shall find.

*Albert F. Bayly**

232

St. Gertrude 65.65. D.

FORWARD through the ages,
In unbroken line,
Move the faithful spirits
At the call divine:
Gifts in differing measure,
Hearts of one accord,
Manifold the service,
One the sure reward.
Forward through the ages,
In unbroken line,
Move the faithful spirits
At the call divine.

Wider grows the kingdom,
Reign of love and light;
For it we must labour,
Till our faith is sight.
Prophets have proclaimed it,
Martyrs testified,
Poets sung its glory,
Brave souls for it died.

Not alone we conquer,
Not alone we fall;
In each loss or triumph
Lose or triumph all.
Bound by God's far purpose
In one living whole,
Move we on together
To the shining goal!

*F. L. Hosmer**

233

Austria 87.87.D

GLORIOUS things of thee are spoken,
  Zion, city of our God;
He whose word cannot be broken
  Formed thee for his own abode.
On the Rock of Ages founded,
  What can shake thy sure repose?
With salvation's walls surrounded,
  Thou mayest smile at all thy foes.

See! The streams of living waters,
  Springing from eternal love,
Well supply thy sons and daughters,
  And all fear of want remove;
Who can faint, while such a river
  Ever flows their thirst to assuage –
Grace, which, like the Lord, the giver,
  Never fails from age to age?

Saviour, if of Zion's city
  I, through grace, a member am,
Let the world deride or pity,
  I will glory in thy name.
Fading is the worldling's pleasure,
  All his boasted pomp and show;
Solid joys and lasting treasure
  None but Zion's children know.

John Newton

234

Westminster Abbey 87.87.87.

BLESSÈD city, heavenly Salem,
  Vision dear of peace and love,
Who of living stones art builded
  In the height of heaven above,
And by angel hosts encircled
  As a bride dost earthward move!

Christ is made the sure foundation,
  Christ the head and corner-stone,
Chosen of the Lord, and precious,
  Binding all the church in one,
Holy Zion's help for ever,
  And her confidence alone.

To this temple, where we call thee,
  Come, O Lord of Hosts, today;
With thy wonted loving-kindness
  Hear thy servants as they pray;
And thy fullest benediction
  Shed within its walls alway.

Here vouchsafe to all thy servants
  What they ask of thee to gain,
What they gain from thee for ever
  With the blessèd to retain,
And hereafter in thy glory
  Evermore with thee to reign.

6th or 7th century
*trans. J. M. Neale**

235

Kilmarnock C.M.

In Christ there is no east or west,
  In him no south or north,
But one great fellowship of love
  Throughout the whole wide earth.

In him shall true hearts everywhere
  Their high communion find,
His service is the golden cord
  Close-binding humankind.

Join hands, then, family of the faith,
  Whate'er your race may be,
Whoever does my Father's will
  Is surely kin to me.

In Christ now meet both east and west.
In him meet south and north,
All Christlike souls are one in him,
Throughout the whole wide earth.

*John Oxenham**
(altered by permission)

236

Tallis' Canon LM

COME, all who look to Christ today,
Stretch out your hands, enlarge your mind,
Together share his living way
Where all who humbly seek will find.

Come, all who will from every race;
Find here new powers of fellowship
Accept the Spirit's strong embrace
Which binds us to the common good.

Come, young and old from every church,
Bring all your treasuries of prayer,
Join the dynamic Spirit's search
To press beyond the truths we share.

Bring your traditions' richest store,
Your hymns and rites and cherished creeds;
Explore our visions, pray for more,
Since God delights to meet fresh needs.

Come, trust in Christ and live in peace,
Anticipate that final light
When strife and bigotry shall cease,
And faith be lost in praise and sight.

*Richard G. Jones**
(altered by permission)

237

Thornbury *76.76.D*

THY hand, O God, has guided
  Thy flock, from age to age;
The wondrous tale is written,
  Full clear, on every page;
Our founders owned thy goodness,
  And we their deeds record;
And both of this bear witness:
  One church, one faith, one Lord.

Thy heralds brought glad tidings
  To greatest, as to least;
They bade all rise, and hasten
  To share the great King's feast;
Their gospel of redemption,
  Sin pardoned, right restored,
Was all in this enfolded:
  One church, one faith, one Lord.

Thy mercy will not fail us,
  Nor leave thy work undone;
With thy right hand to help us,
  The vict'ry shall be won;
And then, in earth and heaven,
  Thy name shall be adored,
And this shall be their anthem:
  One church, one faith, one Lord!

*E. H. Plumptre**

238

Dank sei Gott 76.76.D.

TO us have distant ages
  Bequeathed their noblest thought;
For us have holy sages
  God's hidden wisdom sought;
The truths of ancient teachers
  Still precious to us prove;
The words of ancient preachers
  With sacred passion move.

Not dear their lives accounting,
  The martyrs' blood hath flowed;
Their spirits heavenward mounting
  The path to light have showed;
Sublime their holy daring,
  Its fruits to us belong –
Their faith and freedom sharing,
  Their triumph and their song.

Bright are their deeds in story!
  We hail, with homage due,
The imperishable glory
  Of the brave, the good, the true;
In love their names enshrining,
  We take the blessing given;
Our lives, with theirs entwining,
  We give to truth and heaven.

*S. Wolcott**

239

Solomon C.M.

FROM age to age how grandly rise
  The prophet souls in line!
Above the passing centuries
  Like beacon lights they shine.

Through differing accents of the lip
  One message they proclaim,
One growing bond of fellowship,
  Above all names one Name.

They witness to one heritage,
One Spirit's quickening breath,
One widening reign, from age to age,
Of freedom and of faith.

Their kindling power our souls confess;
Though dead they speak to-day:
How great the cloud of witnesses
Encompassing our way!

Through every race, in every clime,
One song shall yet be heard:
Move onward in thy course sublime,
O everlasting Word!

F. L. Hosmer

240

Dominus Regit Me 87.87.*(iambic)*

NOW praise we thus in song again
The founders named in story;
And praise the Lord who now as then
Reveals in us his glory.

Praise we the wise and brave and strong,
Who graced their generation;
Who helped the right, and fought the wrong,
And made our folk a nation.

Praise we the great of heart and mind,
The singers sweetly gifted,
Whose music like a mighty wind
The souls of all uplifted.

Praise we the peaceful folk of skill
Who builded homes of beauty,
And, rich in art, made richer still
The fellowship of duty.

Praise we the glorious names we know;
And they whose names are perished,
Lost in the haze of long ago –
In silent love be cherished.

In peace their sacred ashes rest,
   Fulfilled their day's endeavour;
They blessed the earth, and they are blessed
   Of God and us for ever.

*W. G. Tarrant**

241

St. Austin/Moscow   664.6664.

ALL hail, God's angel, Truth!
In whose immortal youth
   Fresh graces shine:
To her mild majesty,
Lord, help us bend the knee,
And all her beauty see
      And wealth divine.

Thanks for the names that light
The path of Truth and Right
   And Freedom's way:
For all whose life doth prove
The might of Faith, Hope, Love,
Thousands of hearts to move,
      A power to-day;

Thanks for the hearts of love,
Kin to thine own above,
   Tender and brave;
Ready to bear the cross,
To suffer pain and loss,
And earthly good count dross,
      In toils to save.

May their dear memory be
True guide, O Lord, to thee,
   With saints of old;
And may the work they wrought,
The truth of God they taught,
The good for all they sought,
      Ever unfold!

*W. Newell**

242

Melcombe L.M.

WHEREVER through the ages rise
The altars of self-sacrifice,
Where love its arms has opened wide,
Or for a friend has calmly died,

We see the same white wings outspread
That hovered o'er the Master's head;
And in all lands beneath the sun
The heart affirmeth, "Love is one."

Up from undated time they come,
The holy ranks of martyrdom,
And to the cross and passion bring
Their fellowship of suffering.

And the great marvel of their death
To the one order witnesseth –
Each, in his measure, but a part
Of God's immeasurable heart.

*J. G. Whittier**

243

St. Ethelwald S.M.

FOR all thy saints, O Lord!
Who strove in thee to live,
Who followed thee, obeyed, adored,
Our grateful hymn receive.

For all thy saints, O Lord!
Accept our thankful cry,
Who counted thee their great reward,
And strove in thee to die.

They all, in life and death,
With thee, Lord, in their view,
Learned from thy Holy Spirit's breath
To suffer and to do.

For this thy Name we bless,
And humbly pray that we
May follow them in holiness,
And live and die in thee.

R. Mant

244

Sine nomine 10 10 10.4.

FOR all the saints, who from their labours rest,
Who thee by faith before the world confessed,
Thy name, O Jesus, be for ever blest.
Alleluia!

Thou wast their rock, their fortress, and their might;
Thou, Lord, their Captain in the well-fought fight;
Thou, in the darkness drear, their one true Light.
Alleluia!

O may thy soldiers, faithful, true, and bold,
Fight as the saints who nobly fought of old,
And win, with them, the victor's crown of gold.
Alleluia!

O blest communion, fellowship divine!
We feebly struggle, they in glory shine;
Yet all are one in thee, for all are thine. *Alleluia!*

And when the strife is fierce, the warfare long,
Steals on the ear the distant triumph-song,
And hearts are brave again, and arms are strong.
Alleluia!

The golden evening brightens in the west:
Soon, soon to faithful warriors cometh rest;
Deep is the calm of Paradise the blest.
Alleluia!

*W. W. How**

245

Royal Oak 76.76. with refrain

ALL things bright and beautiful,
All creatures great and small,
All things wise and wonderful –
The Lord God made them all.

Each little flower that opens,
Each little bird that sings,
He made their glowing colours,
He made their tiny wings.

The purple-headed mountain,
The river running by,
The sunset and the morning
That brighten up the sky,

The cold wind in the winter,
The pleasant summer sun,
The ripe fruits in the garden –
He made them every one.

He gave us eyes to see them,
And lips that we might tell
How great is God Almighty,
Who has made all things well.

Cecil Frances Alexander

246

Princethorpe 65.65.D.

EARLY in life's morning,
Lord, we come to thee:
Raise our song of gladness,
Lowly bend the knee;
While the dew still sparkles,
In the woodland ways,
While the freshness lingers,
Hear our hymn of praise.

For the spring we thank thee,
  For the flowers that bloom;
For the new life rising
  From dark winter's tomb;
Birds are singing round us;
  We would also praise,
Hearts and voices blending
  In the song we raise.

Early in life's morning
  May we hear thy call;
While the brightness lingers,
  Ere the shadows fall;
May we yield thee gladly
  All our future days,
So shall our whole lifetime
  Be a song of praise.

Helen Summers

247

Meirionydd/In Memoriam 76.76.D.

THE wise may bring their learning,
  The rich may bring their wealth,
And some may bring their greatness,
  And some bring strength and health;
We too would bring our treasures
  To offer to the King;
We have no wealth or learning;
  What shall we children bring?

We'll bring him hearts that love him;
  We'll bring him thankful praise,
And young souls humbly striving
  To walk in holy ways:
And these shall be the treasures
  We offer to the King,
And these are gifts that even
  The poorest child may bring.

We'll bring the many duties
  We have to do each day;
We'll try our best to please him,
  At home, at school, at play:
And better are these treasures
  To offer to our King
Than richest gifts without them;
  Yet these a child may bring.

Anon.

248

Capel/Rodmell C.M.

GOD make my life a little light
  Within the world to glow;
A little flame that burneth bright,
  Wherever I may go.

God make my life a little flower,
  That giveth joy to all,
Content to bloom in native bower,
  Although the place be small.

God make my life a little song,
  That comforteth the sad;
That helpeth others to be strong,
  And makes the singer glad.

God make my life a little staff,
  Whereon the weak may rest,
That so what health and strength I have
  May serve my neighbour best.

God make my life a little hymn
  Of tenderness and praise;
Of faith that never groweth dim
  In all his wondrous ways.

*Matilda Betham-Edwards**

249

Rodmell C.M.

ALL things which live below the sky,
Or move within the sea,
Are creatures of the Lord most high,
And kindred unto me.

I love to hear the robin sing,
Perched on the highest bough;
To see the rook with purple wing
Follow the shining plough.

I love to watch the swallow skim
The river in his flight;
To mark, when day is growing dim,
The glowworm's silvery light;

The seagull whiter than the foam,
The fish that dart beneath;
The lowing cattle coming home;
The goats upon the heath.

God taught the wren to build her nest,
The lark to soar above,
The hen to gather to her breast
The offspring of her love.

Beneath his heaven there's room for all;
He gives to all their meat;
He sees the meanest sparrow fall
Unnoticed in the street.

Almighty Father, King of kings,
The lover of the meek,
Make me a friend of helpless things,
Defender of the weak.

*E. J. Brailsford**

250

Innocents 77.77.

FATHER, lead me day by day,
Ever in thy loving way;
Teach me to be pure and true,
Show me what I ought to do.

When in danger, make me brave;
Make me know that thou canst save:
Keep me safe by thy dear side;
Let me in thy love abide.

When I'm tempted to do wrong,
Make me steadfast, wise, and strong;
And when all alone I stand,
Shield me with thy mighty hand.

When my heart is full and free,
Help me to remember thee –
Happy most of all to know
That my Father loves me so.

When my work seems hard and dry,
May I press on cheerfully;
Help me patiently to bear
Pain and hardship, toil and care.

May I see the good and bright,
When they pass before my sight;
May I hear the heavenly voice
When the pure and wise rejoice.

May I do the good I know,
Be thy loving child below,
Then at last go home to thee,
Evermore thy child to be.

*J. P. Hopps**

251

Wareham L.M.

O FATHER, thou who givest all
The bounty of thy perfect love,
We thank thee that upon us fall
Such tender blessings from above.

We thank thee for the grace of home,
For mother's love and father's care;
For friends and teachers – all who come
Our joys and hopes and fears to share;

For eyes to see and ears to hear,
For hands to serve and arms to lift,
For shoulders broad and strong to bear,
For feet to run on errands swift;

For faith to conquer doubt and fear
For love to answer every call,
For strength to do, and will to dare,
We thank thee, O thou Lord of all.

J. H. Holmes

252

Mozart 76.76.D. (trochaic)

LOOKING upward day by day,
Sunshine on our faces;
Pressing onward every day
Toward the heavenly places.
Growing every day in awe,
For thy Name is holy;
Learning every day to love
With a love more lowly.

Walking every day more close
To our Elder Brother;
Growing every day more true
Unto one another.
Every day more gratefully
Kindnesses receiving,
Every day more readily
Injuries forgiving.

Leaving every day behind
  Something which might hinder,
Running swifter every day,
  Growing purer, kinder.
Lord so pray we every day,
  Hear us in thy pity,
That we enter in at last
  To the Holy City.

Mary Butler and others

253

Lucerne 87.87.

GOD is good; we come before him
  So that we may sing his praise,
Giving thanks for all his goodness,
  As we learn his wondrous ways.

God is great; we come before him
  So that we may bow in prayer,
Seeking strength to fight our battles,
  Knowing he is everywhere.

God is wise; we come before him
  So that we may know his law,
Learning from the folk before us,
  How to serve him more and more.

*E. Mildred Nevill**

254

Platt's Lane Irregular

GOD who made the earth,
  The air, the sky, the sea,
Who gave the light its birth,
  Careth for me.

God, who made the grass,
  The flower, the fruit, the tree,
The day and night to pass,
  Careth for me.

God who made the sun,
The moon, the stars, is he
Who, when life's clouds come on,
Careth for me.

Sarah B. Rhodes

255

Water End 65.65. Irregular

GLAD that I live am I;
That the sky is blue;
Glad for the country lanes,
And the fall of dew.

After the sun, the rain;
After the rain, the sun;
This is the way of life,
Till the work be done.

All that we need to do,
Be we low or high,
Is to see that we grow
Nearer the sky.

Lizette W. Reese

256

Stowey 74.74. Irregular

WHEN a knight won his spurs in the stories of old,
He was gentle and brave, he was gallant and bold;
With a shield on his arm and a lance in his hand
For God and for valour he rode through the land.

No charger have I, and no sword by my side,
Yet still to adventure and battles I ride,
Though back into storyland giants have fled,
And knights are no more and the dragons are dead.

Let faith be my shield and let joy be my steed
'Gainst the dragons of anger, the ogres of greed;
And let me set free, with the sword of my youth,
From the castle of darkness the power of the truth.

Jan Struther

257

Slane *10 11.11 12*

LORD of all hopefulness, Lord of all joy,
Whose trust, ever childlike, no cares could destroy,
Be there at our waking, and give us, we pray,
Your bliss in our hearts, Lord, at the break of the day.

Lord of all eagerness, Lord of all faith,
Whose strong hands were skilled at the plane and the lathe,
Be there at our labours, and give us, we pray,
Your strength in our hearts, Lord, at the noon of the day.

Lord of all kindliness, Lord of all grace,
Your hands swift to welcome, your arms to embrace,
Be there at our homing, and give us, we pray,
Your love in our hearts, Lord, at the eve of the day.

Lord of all gentleness, Lord of all calm,
Whose voice is contentment, whose presence is balm,
Be there at our sleeping, and give us, we pray,
Your peace in our hearts, Lord, at the end of the day.

Jan Struther

258

Will your anchor hold *10 9. 10 9. with refrain*

WILL your anchor hold in the storms of life,
When the clouds unfold their wings of strife?
When the strong tides lift, and the cables strain,
Will your anchor drift, or firm remain?

We have an anchor that keeps the soul
Steadfast and sure while the billows roll:
Fastened to the rock which cannot move,
Grounded firm and deep in the Saviour's love!

Will your anchor hold in the straits of fear,
When the breakers roar and the reef is near?
While the surges rave, and the wild winds blow,
Shall the angry waves then your barque o'erflow?

Will your anchor hold in the floods of death,
When the waters cold chill your latest breath?
On the rising tide you can never fail,
While your anchor holds within the veil:

Will your eyes behold through the morning light
The city of gold and the harbour bright?
Will you anchor safe by the heavenly shore,
When life's storms are past for evermore?

Priscilla Owens

259

Quem Pastores 888.7

JESUS, good above all other,
Gentle child of gentle mother,
In a stable born our brother,
Give us grace to persevere.

Jesus, cradled in a manger,
For us facing every danger,
Living as a homeless stranger,
Make we thee our King most dear.

Jesus, for thy people dying,
Risen Master, death defying,
Through thy grace, our souls supplying,
Keep us to thy presence near.

Jesus, who our sorrows bearest,
All our thoughts and hopes thou sharest;
Thou to us the truth declarest;
Help us all thy truth to hear.

Lord, in all our doings guide us;
Pride and hate shall ne'er divide us;
We'll go on with thee beside us,
And with joy we'll persevere!

*P. Dearmer**

260

Laredo 12 10.12 11.

THE Church is wherever God's people are praising,
Singing their thanks for joy on this day.
The Church is wherever disciples of Jesus
Remember his story and walk in his way.

The Church is wherever God's people are helping,
Caring for neighbours in sickness and need.
The Church is wherever God's people are sharing
The words of the Bible in gift and in deed.

Carol Rose Ikeler

261

Theodoric 666.66 with refrain

GOD is love: his the care,
Tending each, everywhere.
God is love – all is there!
Jesus came to show him,
That we all might know him:

Sing aloud, loud, loud!
Sing aloud, loud, loud!
God is good!
God is truth!
God is beauty! Praise him!

None can see God above;
Neighbours here we can love;
Thus may we Godward move,
Finding him in others,
Sisters all, and brothers:

Living for humankind,
Jesus death could not bind;
Now he rules heart and mind,
For he came to save us
By the truth he gave us:

To our Lord praise we sing –
Light and life, friend and king,
Here on earth love to bring,
Pattern for our duty,
Showing God in beauty:

*P. Dearmer**

262

Go Tell Everyone Irregular

GOD'S Spirit is in my heart;
He has called me and set me apart.
This is what I have to do –
What I have to do:

He sent me to give the good news to the poor,
Tell prisoners that they are prisoners no more,
Tell blind people that they can see,
And set the down-trodden free,
And go tell everyone
The news that the kingdom of God has come;
And go tell everyone
The news that God's kingdom has come.

Just as the Father sent me,
So I'm sending you out to be
My witness throughout the world –
The whole of the world:

Don't carry a load in your pack;
You don't need two shirts on your back;
A workman can earn his own keep –
Can earn his own keep:

Don't worry what you have to say;
Don't worry, because on that day
God's spirit will speak in your heart –
Will speak in your heart:

Alan T. Dale

263

The beautiful old story/ Deerhurst *87.87.D.*

O THE beautiful old story
Of the little child that lay
In a manger on that morning,
When the stars sang in the day;
When the happy shepherds kneeling,
As before a holy shrine,
Blessed God and the tender mother
For a life that was divine.

O the pleasant, peaceful story
Of the youth who grew so fair,
In his father's humble dwelling,
Poverty and toil to share,
Till around him, in the temple,
Teachers wondered as they heard
In his questioning and answers
Holy wisdom in each word.

O the wonderful, true story
Of the messenger from God,
Who among the poor and lowly
Bravely and devoutly trod,
Working miracles of mercy,
Preaching peace, rebuking strife,
Blessing all the little children,
Lifting up the dead to life.

O the sad and solemn story
Of the cross, the crown, the spear,
Of the pardon, pain and glory
That have made this name so dear.
This example let us follow,
Fearless, faithful to the end,
Walking in the sacred footsteps
Of our Brother, Master,Friend.

Louisa M. Alcott

264

Stuttgart 87.87.

EVER find I joy in reading,
In the ancient holy book,
Of the gentle Teacher's pleading,
Truth in every word and look.

How, when children came, he blessed them,
Suffered no man to reprove:
Took them in his arms, and pressed them
To his heart with words of love.

How no contrite soul e'er sought him
And was bidden to depart;
How with gentle words he taught him,
Soothed and healed the broken heart.

Still I read the ancient story,
And my joy is ever new.
Lord, that I may share his glory,
Make me tender, loving, true!

*Luise Hensel, trans. Catherine Winkworth**

265

Lord of the dance *Irregular*

I DANCED in the morning
When the world was begun,
And I danced in the moon
And the stars and the sun;
And I came down from Heaven
And I danced on the earth,
At Bethlehem
I had my birth.

Dance then, wherever you may be,
I am the Lord of the Dance, said he,
And I'll lead you all wherever you may be,
And I'll lead you all in the Dance, said he.

I danced for the scribe
And the pharisee,
But they would not dance
And they wouldn't follow me.
I danced for the fishermen,
For James and John –
They came with me
And the dance went on.

I danced on the Sabbath
And I cured the lame;
The holy people
Said it was a shame.
They whipped and they stripped
And they hung me on high,
And they left me there
On a Cross to die.

I danced on a Friday
When the sky turned black –
It's hard to dance
With the devil on your back.
They buried my body
And they thought I'd gone,
But I am the dance,
And I still go on.

They cut me down
And I leapt up high;
I am the life
That'll never, never die;
I'll live in you
If you'll live in me –
I am the Lord
Of the Dance, said he.

Sydney Carter

266

Little Cornard 66.66.88.

LORD of the wondrous earth,
Into thy courts we throng,
Seeking to serve with mirth,
Stirring our hearts with song.
O Father-Spirit, touch with power
Our youthful wills, this worship-hour.

Lift from our laden lives
All we have wrought with shame;
Stir every heart that strives,
Tense with unswerving aim,
To consecrate our talent-skill
And with delight our days to fill.

Grant us the vision keen
Brave souls of old time knew;
Faith in the things not seen;
Faith in our strength to do;
That through our seeming-tedious days
Our feet may find the brightest ways.

Daring the truth to speak,
E'en to the worldly-wise;
Swift to defend the weak,
Eager for enterprise,
We steel our wills for sacrifice,
And banish faithless cowardice.

So may our tongues unite
Strong in their glad accord,
Cleaving the zenith-height,
Splendid with song outpoured,
To rouse the nations with our call,
That Youth may serve the Lord of all.

*A. W. Vallance**

267

Chorus Angelorum/St.Saviour C.M.

YOUNG souls, so strong the race to run,
And win each height sublime,
Unweary still would ye march on,
And still exulting climb?

Walk with the Lord! along the road
Your strength he will renew;
Wait on the everlasting God,
And he will wait on you.

Burn with his love! your fading fire
An endless flame will glow;
Life from the Well of Life require!
The stream will ever flow.

Ye shall not faint, ye shall not fail,
Still in the Spirit strong:
Each task divine ye still shall hail,
And blend the exulting song.

Aspiring eyes ye still shall raise,
And heights sublime explore:
Like eagles, ye shall sunward gaze;
Like eagles, heavenward soar.

Your wondrous portion shall be this,
Your life below, above,
Eternal youth, eternal bliss,
And everlasting love.

T. H. Gill

268

Saffron Walden 888.6.

JUST as I am, thine own to be,
My Father, God who lovest me,
To consecrate myself to thee,
Now in my youth I come.

In this glad morning of my day,
My life to give, my vows to pay,
With no reserve and no delay
With all my heart I come.

I would live ever in the light,
I would work ever for the right,
I would serve thee with all my might,
Therefore, to thee I come.

Just as I am, young, strong, and free,
To be the best that I can be
For truth, and righteousness, and thee,
Lord of my life, I come.

Marianne Farningham

269

Bishopthorpe C.M.

LORD, in the fulness of my might
I would for thee be strong;
While runneth o'er each new delight,
To thee should soar my song.

I would not give the world my heart,
And then profess thy love;
I would not feel my strength depart,
And then thy service prove.

I would not with swift-wingèd zeal
On the world's errands go,
And labour up the heavenly hill
With weary feet and slow.

O not for thee my weak desires,
My poorer, baser part!
O not for thee my fading fires,
The ashes of my heart!

O choose me in my golden time!
In my dear joys have part!
For thee the glory of my prime –
The fulness of my heart.

I cannot, Lord, too early take
The covenant divine:
Oh, ne'er the happy heart may break
Whose earliest love was thine.

T. H. Gill

270

Lübeck 77.77.

LIGHT of Ages, may thy ray
Guide our feet upon the way,
And the clouds and mists disperse
As thou didst in former years.

Light of conscience, clear and still,
Be a beacon to our will;
Like the steadfast northern light,
Guide us in the deepest night.

Light of knowledge, spread and grow
As the dawn to noon-day glow;
Kindle in our heart of youth
Passion for the perfect truth.

Light of love, O may thy fire
Purify our soul's desire,
And unite us, heart and mind,
As we serve all humankind.

Light of martyrs, prophets, seers,
Gird our hearts against all fears;
Pledge we then our loyalty
And the daring to be free.

*P. Chubb**

271

Wolvercote / Thornbury 76.76.D.

O JESUS, I have promised
  To serve thee to the end;
Be thou for ever near me,
  My master and my friend;
I shall not fear the battle
  If thou art by my side,
Nor wander from the pathway
  If thou wilt be my guide.

O let me feel thee near me;
  The world is ever near;
I see the sights that dazzle,
  The tempting sounds I hear;
My foes are ever near me,
  Around me and within;
But, Jesus, draw thou nearer,
  And shield my soul from sin.

O let me hear thee speaking
  In accents clear and still,
Above the storms of passion,
  The murmurs of self-will;
O speak to reassure me,
  To hasten or control;
O speak, and make me listen,
  Thou guardian of my soul.

O Jesus, thou hast promised
  To all who follow thee,
That where thou art in glory
  There shall thy servant be;
And, Jesus, I have promised
  To serve thee to the end;
O give me grace to follow
  My master and my friend!

J. E. Bode

272

Seek Ye First   Irregular

SEEK ye first the kingdom of God,
  And his righteousness,
And all these things shall be added unto you;
  Allelu–, Alleluia:
  Alleluia, Alleluia, Alleluia,
  Allelu–, Alleluia!

Ask, and it shall be given unto you;
  Seek, and ye shall find;
Knock, and the door shall be opened unto you;
  Allelu–, Alleluia:

Man shall not live by bread alone,
  But by every word
That proceeds from the mouth of the Lord;
  Allelu–, Alleluia:

Karen Lafferty

DEDICATION – GENERAL

273

Rockingham   L.M.

THOU Lord of Hosts, whose guiding hand
  Has brought us here before thy face,
Our spirits wait for thy command,
Our silent hearts implore thy peace.

Again we lay their noblest powers,
As offerings, on thy holy shrine;
Thine was the strength that nourished ours;
The soldiers of the Cross are thine.

While watching on our arms at night,
We saw thine angels round us move;
We heard thy call, we felt thy light,
And followed, trusting to thy love.

And now, with hymn and prayer, we stand
To give our strength to thee, great God!
We would redeem thy holy land,
That land which sin so long has trod.

Send us where'er thou wilt, O Lord,
Through rugged toil and wearying fight;
Thy conquering love shall be our sword,
And faith in thee our truest might.

Send down thy constant aid, we pray,
Be thy pure angels with us still;
Thy truth, be that our firmest stay;
Our only rest, to do thy will.

O. B. Frothingham

274

St. Fulbert C.M.

O GOD, whose law is in the sky,
Whose light is on the sea,
Who livest in the human heart,
We give ourselves to thee.

In fearless, world-wide search for truth,
Whatever form it wear,
Or crown or cross, or fame or blame,
We thine ourselves declare.

In love that humankind makes one,
That serves all those in need,
Whose law is helpful sympathy –
In this we're thine indeed.

In labour, whose far-distant end
Is bringing to accord
The earthly fact and seer's dream,
We follow thee, O Lord!

To truth, to love, to duty, then,
Wherever we may be,
We give ourselves; and, doing this,
We give ourselves to thee.

*M. J. Savage**

275

Song 1 *10 10.10 10.10 10.*

ETERNAL Ruler of the ceaseless round
Of circling planets singing on their way;
Guide of the nations from the night profound
Into the glory of the perfect day;
Rule in our hearts that we may ever be
Guided and strengthened and upheld by thee.

We are of thee, the children of thy love,
The kindred of thy well-belovèd Son;
Descend, O Holy Spirit, like a dove,
Into our hearts, that we may be as one,
As one with thee, to whom we ever tend;
As one with him, our Brother and our Friend.

We would be one in hatred of all wrong,
One in our love of all things just and fair;
One with the joy that breaketh into song,
One with the grief that trembles into prayer;
One in the power that makes thy children free
To follow truth, and thus to follow thee.

Oh, clothe us with thy heavenly armour, Lord,
Thy trusty shield, thy sword of love divine!
Our inspiration be thy constant word:
We ask no victories that are not thine.
Give or withhold, let pain or pleasure be,
Enough to know that we are serving thee.

*J. W. Chadwick**

276

St. Margaret *88.88.6.*

O LOVE that wilt not let me go,
I rest my weary soul in thee;
I give thee back the life I owe,
That in thine ocean depths its flow
May richer, fuller be.

O Light that followest all my way,
  I yield my flickering torch to thee;
My heart restores its borrowed ray,
That in thy sunshine's blaze its day
  May brighter, fairer be.

O Joy that seekest me through pain,
  I cannot close my heart to thee;
I trace the rainbow through the rain,
And feel the promise is not vain
  That morn shall tearless be.

O Cross that liftest up my head,
  I dare not ask to fly from thee;
I lay in dust life's glory dead,
And from the ground there blossoms red
  Life that shall endless be.

G. Matheson

277

Ephraim 77.77.

GOD of Truth, we all should be
Firmly grounded upon thee;
Ever on the rock abide,
High above the changing tide.

Ours then the unwavering mind,
No more tossed with every wind;
No more does our steadfast heart
From the living God depart.

Father, strengthen thou my will,
With thy gracious purpose fill;
Rooted, grounded may I be,
Fixed in thy stability.

Henceforth may I firmly stand,
Build no longer on the sand;
But defy temptation's shock,
Firmly founded on the rock.

*S. Longfellow**

278

Thornbury 76.76.D.

O STAR of Truth, down shining
  Through clouds of doubt and fear,
I ask but 'neath thy guidance
  My pathway may appear.
However long the journey,
  How hard soe'er it be,
Though I be lone and weary,
  Lead on, I'll follow thee!

I know thy blessèd radiance
  Can never lead astray,
However ancient custom
  May tread some other way.
E'en if through untrod deserts,
  Or over trackless sea,
Though I be lone and weary,
  Lead on, I'll follow thee!

The bleeding feet of martyrs
  Thy toilsome road have trod;
But fires of human passion
  May light the way to God.
Then, though my feet should falter,
  While I thy beams can see,
Though I be lone and weary,
  Lead on, I'll follow thee!

Though loving friends forsake me,
  Or plead with me in tears;
Though angry foes may threaten
  To shake my soul with fears,
Still to my high allegiance
  I must not faithless be;
Through life, or death, for ever,
  Lead on, I'll follow thee.

M. J. Savage

279

Monks Gate 65.65.6665.

WHO would true valour see,
Let him come hither;
One here will constant be
Come wind, come weather.
There's no discouragement
Shall make him once relent
His first avowed intent
To be a pilgrim.

Whoso beset him round
With dismal stories,
Do but themselves confound:
His strength the more is.
No lion can him fright,
He'll with a giant fight,
But he will have a right
To be a pilgrim.

Hobgoblin nor foul fiend
Can daunt his spirit:
He knows he at the end
Shall life inherit.
Then fancies fly away,
He'll fear not what men say,
He'll labour night and day
To be a pilgrim.

John Bunyan

280

Monks Gate 65.65.6665.

WE who would valiant be
'Gainst all disaster,
Let us in constancy
Follow the Master.
There's no discouragement
Shall make us once relent
Our first avowed intent
To be a pilgrim.

Whoso beset us round
  With dismal stories,
Do but themselves confound –
  Our strength the more is.
No foes shall stay our might,
However fierce the fight:
We will make good our right
  To be a pilgrim.

Since, Lord, thou dost defend
  Us with thy Spirit,
We know we at the end
  Shall life inherit.
Then fancies flee away!
We'll fear not what men say,
We'll labour night and day
  To be a pilgrim.

John Bunyan and others

281

St. Patrick L.M.D.

I BIND unto myself to-day
  The virtues of the star-lit heaven,
The glorious sun's life-giving ray,
  The whiteness of the moon at even,
The flashing of the lightning free,
  The whirling wind's tempestuous shocks,
The stable earth, the deep salt sea,
  Around the old eternal rocks.

I bind unto myself to-day
  The power of God to hold and lead,
His eye to watch, his might to stay,
  His ear to hearken to my need.
The wisdom of my God to teach,
  His hand to guide, his shield to ward;
The word of God to give me speech,
  His heavenly host to be my guard.

St. Patrick, trans. Cecil Frances Alexander

282

Woodlands 10 10.10 10.

"LIFT up your hearts!" We lift them, Lord, to thee;
Here at thy feet none other may we see:
"Lift up your hearts!" E'en so, with one accord
We lift them up, we lift them to the Lord.

Above the level of the former years,
The mire of sin, the slough of guilty fears,
The mist of doubt, the blight of love's decay,
O Lord of Light, lift all our hearts to-day!

Above the swamps of subterfuge and shame,
The deeds, the thoughts, that honour may not name,
The halting tongue that dares not tell the whole,
O Lord of Truth, lift every Christian soul!

Lift every gift that thou thyself hast given;
Low lies the best till lifted up to heaven:
Low lie the bounding heart, the teeming brain,
Till, sent from God, they mount to God again.

Then, as the trumpet-call, in after years,
"Lift up your hearts!" rings pealing in our ears,
Still shall those hearts respond, with full accord,
"We lift them up, we lift them to the Lord!"

H. M. Butler

283

Nottingham 77.77.

TAKE my life, and let it be
Consecrated, Lord, to thee;
Take my moments, and my days,
Let them flow in ceaseless praise.

Take my hands, and let them move
With the impulse of thy love;
Take my feet, and let them be
Swift and beautiful for thee.

Take my voice, and let me sing
Always, only, for my King;
Take my lips, and let them be
Filled with messages from thee.

Take my will, and make it thine;
It shall be no longer mine;
Take my heart, it is thine own,
It shall be thy royal throne.

Take my love, my Lord; I pour
At thy feet its treasure-store;
Take myself, and I will be
Ever, only, all for thee.

Frances Ridley Havergal

284

Magda 10 10.10 10.

FATHER in heaven, we wait before thy face,
Grant us, we pray, thy presence in this place;
Send down to longing hearts who seek thee here,
The message of thy love, which knows no fear.

Grant us the tongues of fire that fell of old,
The vision clear that made thy prophets bold,
The open mind, the high and pure intent,
The strenuous will on selfless service bent.

Grant us amid the shadows of our years
The inner peace that conquers grief and tears;
Teach us the holy secret Jesus saw,
The soul's beatitude, the perfect law.

O living God, we need thy help and power
To consecrate the purpose of this hour:
Grant us the shield of faith, the sword of light;
Then send us forth to battle for the right.

F. Phalen

285

Slane *10 10.10 10. (dactylic)*

BE thou my Vision, O Lord of my heart;
  Naught be all else to me, save that thou art;
Thou my best thought, by day or by night,
  Waking or sleeping, thy presence my light.

Be thou my wisdom and thou my true word;
  I ever with thee and thou with me, Lord;
Thou my great Father, I thy true child;
  Thou in me dwelling, I with thee reconciled.

Be thou my breastplate, my sword for the fight,
  Be thou my dignity, thou my delight.
Thou my soul's shelter, thou my high tower:
  Raise thou me heavenward, O power of my power.

Riches I heed not, nor false empty praise,
  Thou mine inheritance, now and always:
Thou and thou only, first in my heart,
  High King of heaven, my treasure thou art.

High King of heaven, my victory won,
  May I reach heaven's joys, O bright heaven's Sun!
Heart of my own heart, whatever befall,
  Still be my vision, O Ruler of all.

Ancient Irish,
trans. M. E. Byrne and E. H. Hull

286

Gatescarth *86.886.*

GIVE to me, Lord, a thankful heart
And a discerning mind;
Give, as I play the Christian's part,
The strength to finish what I start
  And act on what I find.

When, in the rush of days, my will
  Is habit-bound and slow,
Help me to keep in vision, still,
What love and power and peace can fill
  A life that trusts in you.

By your divine and urgent claim,
  And by your human face,
Kindle our sinking hearts to flame,
And as you teach the world your name
  Let it become your place.

Jesus, with all your church I long
  To see your kingdom come:
Show me your way of righting wrong
And turning sorrow into song
  Until you bring me home.

Caryl Micklem

287

Hereford L.M.

O THOU, who deignest from above
The pure celestial fire to impart,
Kindle a flame of sacred love
On the mean altar of my heart.

There let it for thy glory burn,
With inextinguishable blaze;
And trembling to its source return
In humble prayer and fervent praise.

O Lord, confirm my heart's desire,
To work, and speak, and think for thee;
Still let me guard the holy fire,
And still stir up thy gift in me;

Ready for all thy perfect will,
My acts of faith and love repeat;
Till death thy endless mercies seal,
And make the sacrifice complete.

*Charles Wesley**

288

Rimington L.M.

JESUS shall reign where'er the sun
Doth his successive journeys run;
His kingdom stretch from shore to shore,
Till moons shall wax and wane no more.

For him shall endless prayer be made,
And praises throng to crown his head;
His name like sweet perfume shall rise
With every morning sacrifice;

People and realms of every tongue
Dwell on his love with sweetest song;
And infant voices shall proclaim
Their early blessings on his name.

Blessings abound where'er he reigns;
The prisoner leaps to lose his chains;
The weary find eternal rest,
And all who are in want are blest.

Let all God's creatures rise and bring
Their special honours to our King;
Angels descend with songs again,
And earth repeat the loud amen.

*Isaac Watts**

CHRISTIAN WORK AND SERVICE

289

Carlisle S.M.

GOD of the earnest heart,
The trust assured and still,
Thou who our strength for ever art,
We come to do thy will.

Upon the painful road
By saints serenely trod,
Whereon their hallowing influence flowed,
Would we go forth, O God!

To draw thy blessing down,
And bring the wronged redress,
To give this glorious world its crown –
The spirit's godlikeness.

No dreams from toil to charm,
No trembling on the tongue:
Lord, in thy rest may we be calm,
Through thy completeness, strong!

Thou hearest while we pray;
O deep within us write,
With kindling power, our God, to-day,
Thy word – "On earth be Light."

S. Johnson

290

Samson *L.M.*

AWAKE, our souls! away our fears!
Let every trembling thought be gone!
Awake, and run the heavenly race,
And put a cheerful courage on.

True, 'tis a strait and thorny road,
And mortal spirits tire and faint;
But they forget the mighty God,
That feeds the strength of every saint:

The mighty God whose matchless power
Is ever new and ever young,
And firm endures, while endless years
Their everlasting circles run.

From thee, the over-flowing spring,
Our souls shall drink a fresh supply;
While such as trust their native strength
Shall melt away, and droop and die.

Swift as an eagle cuts the air,
We'll mount aloft to thine abode:
On wings of love our souls shall fly,
Nor tire amidst the heavenly road.

Isaac Watts

291

Melcombe L.M.

NOT always on the mount may we
Rapt in the heavenly vision be;
The shores of thought and feeling know
The Spirit's tidal ebb and flow.

Lord, it is good abiding here,
We cry, the heavenly Presence near;
The vision vanishes, our eyes
Are lifted into vacant skies.

Yet has one such exalted hour
Upon the soul redeeming power,
And in its strength through after days
We travel our appointed ways;

Till all the lowly vale grows bright,
Transfigured in remembered light,
And in untiring souls we bear
The freshness of the upper air.

The mount for vision, but below
The paths of daily duty go,
And holier life therein shall own
The pattern on the mountain shown.

*F. L. Hosmer**

292

All for Jesus 87.87.

TELL me not in mournful numbers,
"Life is but an empty dream!"
For the soul is dead that slumbers,
And things are not what they seem.

Life is real! Life is earnest!
And the grave is not its goal;
"Dust thou art, to dust returnest,"
Was not spoken of the soul.

Not enjoyment, and not sorrow,
Is our destined end or way;
But to act that each to-morrow
Find us further than to-day.

Lives of great souls all remind us
We can make our lives sublime,
And, departing, leave behind us
Footprints on the sands of time:

Footprints, that perhaps another
Sailing o'er life's solemn main,
A forlorn and shipwrecked brother,
Seeing, shall take heart again.

Let us then be up and doing,
With a heart for any fate;
Still achieving, still pursuing,
Learn to labour and to wait.

*H. W. Longfellow**

293

Tynemouth/Spohr *86.86.86.*

DISMISS us not thy service, Lord,
But train us for thy will;
For even we in fields so broad,
Some duties may fulfil;
And we will ask for no reward,
Except to serve thee still.

All works are good, and each is best
As most it pleases thee;
Each worker pleases when the rest
Are served in charity;
And neither us nor work unblest
Wilt thou permit to be.

Our Master all the work hath done
He asks of us to-day;
Sharing his service, every one
Share too his sonship may:
Lord, we would serve, and work begun,
Dismiss us not, we pray.

*T. T. Lynch**

294

Salford/St. Denio 11 11.11 11.

"Go work in my vineyard, my garden and field,
And bring me the fruits and the flowers they yield."
The voice of the Master the labourers heard,
And into his harvest they went at his word.

The forebears belovèd, their reaping all done,
Have brought home their sheaves, and their harvest is won;
But lo! as he calleth the weary to sleep,
New harvests arise and new harvesters reap.

The old world rejoiceth again in her youth,
And yieldeth her increase of beauty and truth;
While over the meadows, in sunshine and rain,
The hymn of the labourers riseth again:

"Oh, not to our glory the chorus we raise,
But unto our God be thanksgiving and praise,
For lives growing fruitful, wherever they stand,
And souls that like blossoms make lovely the land.

"O Teacher of teachers and Helper of all,
Thou knowest our need, and thou hearest our call –
Give strength to thy servants their task to fulfil,
And send forth, we pray thee, more labourers still."

*W. G. Tarrant**

295

St. Saviour C.M.

O STILL in accents clear and strong
  Sounds forth the ancient word,
"More reapers for white harvest fields,
  More labourers for the Lord!"

We hear the call; in dreams no more
  In selfish ease we lie,
But, girded for our Father's work,
  Go forth beneath his sky.

Where prophets' word, and martyrs' blood,
  And prayers of saints were sown,
We, to their labours entering in,
  Would reap where they have strown.

O thou, whose call our hearts has stirred,
  To do thy will we come;
Thrust in our sickles at thy word,
  And bear our harvest home.

*S. Longfellow**

296

Simeon L.M.

NOW is the seed-time; God alone
Beholds the end of what is sown;
Beyond our vision weak and dim
The harvest time is hid with him.

It may not be our lot to wield
The sickle in the ripened field,
Nor ours to hear on summer eves
The reaper's song among the sheaves;

Yet where our duty's task is wrought
In unison with God's great thought,
The near and future blend in one,
And whatsoe'er is willed, is done!

Who calls the glorious labour hard?
Who deems it not its own reward?
Who, for its trials, counts it less
A cause of praise and thankfulness?

Be ours the grateful service whence
Comes, day by day, the recompense –
The hope, the trust, the purpose stayed,
The fountain and the noon-day shade.

And unforgotten where it lies,
The seed of generous sacrifice,
Though seeming in the desert cast,
Shall rise with bloom and fruit at last.

*J. G. Whittier**

297

Niagara L.M.

THEY live the longest who live well;
All else is life but flung away;
They live the longest who can tell
Of true things truly done each day.

Be what thou seemest; live thy creed;
Hold up to earth the torch divine;
Be what thou prayest to be made;
Let the great Master's steps be thine.

Fill up each hour with what will last;
Use well the moments as they go;
The life above, when this is past,
Is the ripe fruit of life below.

Sow truth, if thou the true wouldst reap;
Who sows the false shall reap the vain;
Erect and sound thy conscience keep,
From hollow words and deeds refrain.

Sow love, and taste its fruitage pure;
Sow peace, and reap its harvest bright;
Sow sunbeams on the rock and moor,
And find a harvest-home of light.

*H. Bonar**

298

Mirfield C.M.

WHEN courage fails, and faith burns low,
And all are timid grown,
Hold fast thy loyalty, and know
That Truth still moveth on.

For unseen messengers she hath
To work her will and ways,
And even human scorn and wrath
God turneth to her praise.

She can both meek and sovereign be,
In heavenly might secure;
With her is pledge of victory,
And patience to endure.

The race is not unto the swift,
Nor battle to the strong,
When dawn her judgment-days that sift
The claims of right and wrong.

Who follow her, though all deride,
In her strength shall be strong,
Shall see their shame become their pride,
And share her triumph-song!

*F. L. Hosmer**

299

Sussex 87.87.

FATHER, hear the prayer we offer:
Not for ease that prayer shall be,
But for strength that we may ever
Live our lives courageously.

Not for ever in green pastures
Do we ask our way to be;
But by steep and rugged pathways
Would we strive to climb to thee.

Not for ever by still waters
Would we idly quiet stay;
But would win the living fountains
From the rocks along our way.

Be our strength in hours of weakness,
In our wanderings be our guide;
Through endeavour, failure, danger,
Father, be thou at our side.

Let our path be bright or dreary,
Storm or sunshine be our share;
May our souls, in hope unweary,
Make thy work our ceaseless prayer.

*Love Maria Willis**

300

Sandys S.M.

TEACH me, my God and King,
In all things thee to see,
And what I do in anything
To do it as for thee.

A man that looks on glass
On it may stay his eye;
Or if he pleaseth, through it pass,
And then the heaven espy.

All may of thee partake:
Nothing can be so mean,
Which, with this tincture, "For thy sake,"
Will not grow bright and clean.

A servant with this clause
Makes drudgery divine:
Who sweeps a room, as for thy laws,
Makes that and the action fine.

This is the famous stone
That turneth all to gold:
For that which God doth touch and own
Cannot for less be told.

George Herbert

301

Metzler's Redhead C.M.

SCORN not the slightest word or deed,
Nor deem it void of power;
There's fruit in each wind-wafted seed
That waits its natal hour.

A whispered word may touch the heart,
And call it back to life;
A look of love bid sin depart,
And still unholy strife.

No act falls fruitless; none can tell
How vast its power may be,
Nor what results infolded dwell
Within it silently.

Work on, despair not; bring thy mite,
Nor care how small it be;
God is with all that serve the right,
The holy, true, and free.

T. Hincks

302

Tiverton C.M.

O IT is hard to work for God,
To rise and take his part
Upon this battle-field of earth,
And not sometimes lose heart!

He hides himself so wondrously,
As though there were no God;
He is least seen where all the powers
Of ill are most abroad.

Thrice blest is one to whom is given
The instinct that can tell
That God is on the field when he
Is most invisible.

Muse on his justice, downcast soul!
  Muse, and take better heart;
Back with thine angel to the field,
  And bravely do thy part.

For right is right, since God is God;
  And right the day must win;
To doubt would be disloyalty,
  To falter would be sin.

*F. W. Faber**

303

Missionary/Morning Light 76.76.D.

THE voice of God is calling
  Its summons unto men;
As once he spoke in Zion,
  So now he speaks again.
Whom shall I send to succour
  My people in their need?
Whom shall I send to loosen
  The bonds of shame and greed?

I hear my people crying
  In cot and mine and slum;
No field or mart is silent,
  No city street is dumb.
I see my people falling,
  In darkness and despair.
Whom shall I send to shatter
  The fetters which they wear?

We heed, O Lord, thy summons,
  And answer: Here are we!
Send us upon thine errand;
  Let us thy servants be.
Our strength is dust and ashes,
  Our years a passing hour,
But thou canst use our weakness
  To magnify thy power.

From ease and plenty save us,
From pride of place absolve;
Purge us of low desire,
Lift us to high resolve.
Take us, and make us holy,
Teach us thy will and way,
Speak, and, behold, we answer,
Command, and we obey!

J. H. Holmes

304

Tudor C.M.

O YE who, with undoubting eyes,
Through cloud and gathering storm,
Behold the span of freedom's skies,
And sunshine soft and warm –

Press bravely onward! Not in vain
Your trust in human-kind:
The good which bloodshed could not gain,
Your peaceful zeal shall find.

The great hearts of your olden time
Are beating with you strong;
All holy memories and sublime
And glorious round you throng.

The truths ye urge are borne abroad
By every wind and tide;
The voice of Nature and of God
Speaks out upon your side.

The weapons which your hands have found
Are those which heaven has wrought,
Light, Truth, and Love; your battle-ground
The free, broad field of Thought.

*J. G. Whittier**

305

Orient 77.77.

CHRISTIAN, rise and act thy creed,
Let thy prayer be in thy deed;
Seek the right, perform the true,
Raise thy work and life anew.

Hearts around thee sink with care;
Thou canst help their load to bear,
Thou canst bring inspiring light,
Arm their faltering wills to fight.

Wrong shall die in open day,
Virtue shine beyond decay,
Falsehood flee from candour's face,
Health reflect eternal grace.

Let thine alms be hope and joy,
And thy worship God's employ;
Give him thanks in humble zeal,
Learning all his will to feel.

Come then, law divine, and reign,
Freest faith assailed in vain,
Perfect love bereft of fear,
Born in heaven and radiant here!

R. Russell

306

Martyrdom C.M.

OUR Father, while our hearts unlearn
The creeds that wrong thy name,
Still let our hallowed altars burn
With faith's undying flame.

Not by the lightning gleams of wrath
Our souls thy face shall see;
The star of love must light the path
That leads to heaven and thee.

Help us to read our Master's will
Through every darkening stain
That clouds his sacred image still,
And see him once again –

The brother Man, the pitying Friend,
Who weeps for human woes,
Whose pleading words of pardon blend
With cries of raging foes.

If 'mid the gathering storms of doubt
Our hearts grow faint and cold,
The strength we cannot live without
Thy love will not withhold.

Our prayers accept; our sins forgive;
Our youthful zeal renew;
Shape for us holier lives to live,
And nobler work to do.

O. W. Holmes

307

Cromer/Whitburn *L.M.*

LORD, speak to me, that I may speak
In living echoes of thy tone;
As thou hast sought, so let me seek
Thy erring children, lost and lone.

O lead me, Lord, that I may lead
The wandering and the wavering feet;
O feed me, Lord, that I may feed
Thy hungering ones with manna sweet.

O strengthen me, that while I stand
Firm on the rock and strong in thee,
I may stretch out a loving hand
To wrestlers with the troubled sea.

O teach me, Lord, that I may teach
The precious things thou dost impart;
And wing my words, that they may reach
The hidden depths of many a heart.

O fill me with thy fulness, Lord,
Until my very heart o'erflow
In kindling thought and glowing word,
Thy love to tell, thy praise to show.

Frances Ridley Havergal

308

Streatham *66.86.86.*

THOU must be true thyself,
 If thou the truth wouldst teach;
Thy soul must overflow, if thou
 Another's soul wouldst reach.
The overflow of heart it needs
 To give the lips full speech.

Think truly, and thy thoughts
 Shall the world's famine feed;
Speak truly, and each word of thine
 Shall be a fruitful seed;
Live truly, and thy life shall be
 A great and noble creed.

H. Bonar

309

Cwm Rhondda *87.87.87.*

FOR the healing of the nations,
 God, we pray with one accord;
For a just and equal sharing
 Of the things that earth affords.
To a life of love in action
 Help us rise and pledge our word,
 Help us rise and pledge our word.

Lead us ever into freedom,
 From despair your world release;
That, redeemed from war and hatred,
 All may come and go in peace.
Show us how through care and goodness
 Fear will die and hope increase,
 Fear will die and hope increase.

All that kills abundant living,
Let it from the earth depart;
Pride of status, race or schooling,
Dogmas keeping us apart.
May our common quest for justice
Be our brief life's hallowed art,
Be our brief life's hallowed art.

Fred Kaan

310

Faces / Christus der ist mein leben 76.76.

THE faces of the children
Struck down by poverty,
Retarded, starved, exploited,
Are precious, Lord, to thee.

The faces of young people,
Despairing, unemployed,
Street-dwellers on the margins,
Lord, save them from the void.

The faces of our neighbours
Despised because of race,
Rejected sisters, brothers,
Lord, touch them with your grace.

The faces of the workers
Crushed by inhuman toil,
Of landless, homeless peasants:
Lord, their oppressors foil.

The faces of the vagrants,
The jobless, rootless poor,
As hearts grow hard against them,
You cherish them the more.

The faces of the old folk,
The sick, the blind, the lame
Cry out for love, for caring;
In answer, Lord, you came.

The faces of your people,
Their anguish, pain and need,
If we but humbly heed them,
We will serve you indeed.

Clifford Martin Reed

311

Abbot's Leigh 87.87.D.

THOSE who love and those who labour follow in the way of Christ
Thus the first disciples found him, thus the gift of love sufficed.
Jesus says to those who seek him, I will never pass thee by;
Raise the stone and thou shalt find me; cleave the wood, and there am I.

Where the many work together, they with God himself abide.
But the lonely workers also find him ever at their side.
Lo, the Prince of common welfare dwells within the market strife;
Lo, the bread of heaven is broken in the sacrament of life.

Let the seekers never falter till they find themselves afar
With the wisdom of the ages underneath a giant star,
With the richest and the poorest, of the sum of things possessed,
Like a child at first to wonder, like a monarch then to rest.

*Geoffrey Dearmer**
(altered by permission)

312

Ladywell C.M.D.

OUR Father! Thy dear name doth show
  The greatness of thy love;
All are thy children here below
  As in thy heaven above.
One family on earth we are
  Whate'er our race may be;
O help us always to declare
  Our one humanity.

Alike we share thy tender care;
  We trust one heavenly Friend;
Before one mercy-seat in prayer
  In confidence we bend;
Alike we hear thy loving call,
  One heavenly vision see –
One Lord, one faith, one hope for all:
  Our one humanity.

Bring in, we pray, the glorious day
  When battle cries are stilled,
When bitter strife is swept away
  And hearts with love are filled.
Help us to banish pride and wrong,
  Which since earth came to be
Have marred its peace – help to make strong
  Our one humanity.

Close knit the bonds of unity
  That make the whole world one;
Our discords change to harmony
  Like angel-songs begun;
At last, upon that brighter shore,
  Complete thy love's decree,
And heaven shall crown for evermore
  Our one humanity.

*C. H. Richards**

313

Epsom C.M.

TO Mercy, Pity, Peace, and Love
All pray in their distress,
And to these virtues of delight
Return their thankfulness.

For Mercy, Pity, Peace, and Love
Is God our Father dear;
And Mercy, Pity, Peace, and Love
Is man, his child and care.

For Mercy has a human heart;
Pity, a human face;
And Love, the human form divine;
And Peace, the human dress.

Then every man, of every clime,
That prays in his distress,
Prays to the human form divine:
Love, Mercy, Pity, Peace.

William Blake

314

Cuttle Mills/Stephanos 85.83.

WHEN thy heart, with joy o'erflowing,
Sings a thankful prayer,
In thy joy, O let thy neighbours
With thee share.

When the harvest sheaves ingathered
Fill thy barns with store,
To thy God and to thy neighbours
Give the more.

If thy soul, with power uplifted,
Yearn for glorious deed,
Give thy strength to serve thy neighbours
In their need.

Hast thou borne a secret sorrow
In thy lonely breast?
Take to thee thy sorrowing neighbour
For a guest;

Share with all thy bread of blessing,
Sorrow's burden share;
When thy heart enfolds thy neighbours,
God is there.

*T.C.Williams**

315

Rockingham L.M.

THOU Gracious Power, whose mercy lends
The light of home, the smile of friends,
Our gathered flock thine arms enfold
As in the peaceful days of old.

Wilt thou not hear us while we raise,
In one accord of solemn praise,
The voices that have mingled long
In joyous flow of mirth and song?

For all the blessings life has brought,
For all its sorrowing hours have taught,
For all we mourn, for all we keep,
The hands we clasp, the loved that sleep;

The noontide sunshine of the past,
These brief, bright moments fading fast,
The stars that gild our darkening years,
The twilight ray from holier spheres:

We thank thee, Father! let thy grace
Our loving circle still embrace,
Thy mercy shed its heavenly store,
Thy peace be with us evermore!

*O. W. Holmes**

316

Mendip/St. Fulbert C.M.

MAKE channels for the streams of love,
Where they may broadly run;
For love has overflowing streams
To fill them every one.

But if at any time we cease
Such channels to provide,
The very founts of love for us
Will soon be parched and dried.

For we must share if we would keep
That blessing from above;
Ceasing to give we cease to have –
This is the law of love.

R. C. Trench

317

St. Fulbert C.M.

O HELP the prophet to be bold,
The poet to be true!
It yet remains for us to learn
What love to all may do,

With faith not pent within a book,
Or buried in a creed,
But growing with the expanding thought
And deepening with the need:

A faith whose sacred strength is sure,
And needs no priest to tell;
Its law – "Be kind, be pure, be just,"
Its promise – "Thence be well."

For joy shall one with feeling be,
And feeling, planet-wide,
Where many folk have done their best,
And, doing it, have died.

O help the prophet to be bold,
The poet to be true!
It yet remains for us to learn
What love to all may do.

*L. Guggenberger**

318

St. Bees 77.77.

CAN I see another's woe,
And not be in sorrow too?
Can I see another's grief,
And not seek for kind relief?

Can I see a falling tear,
And not feel my sorrow's share?
Can a father see his child
Weep, nor be with sorrow filled?

Can a mother sit and hear
Infant groan, an infant fear?
No, no, never can it be!
Never, never can it be!

William Blake

319

When I needed a neighbour 13.10. with refrain

WHEN I needed a neighbour, were you there, were you there?
When I needed a neighbour, were you there?
And the creed and the colour and the name won't matter,
Were you there?

I was hungry and thirsty, were you there, were you there?
I was hungry and thirsty, were you there?

I was cold, I was naked, were you there, were you there?
I was cold, I was naked , were you there?

When I needed a shelter, were you there, were you there?
When I needed a shelter, were you there?

When I needed a healer, were you there, were you there?
When I needed a healer, were you there?

When they put me in prison, were you there, were you there?
When they put me in prison, were you there?

Wherever you travel, I'll be there, I'll be there,
Wherever you travel, I'll be there.

And the creed and the colour and the name won't matter,
I'll be there,

Sydney Carter

320

Beulah C.M.D.

THE rose is queen among the flowers,
None other is so fair;
The lily nodding on her stem
With fragrance fills the air.
But sweeter than the lily's breath
And than the rose more fair,
The tender love of human hearts,
That springeth everywhere.

The rose will fade and fall away,
The lily, too, will die;
But love shall live for evermore
Beyond the starry sky.
Then sweeter than the lily's breath,
And than the rose more fair,
The tender love of human hearts,
Upspringing everywhere.

F. L. Hosmer

321

St.Oswald 87.87.

HEAVEN is here, where hymns of gladness
Cheer the toiler's rugged way,
In this world where clouds of sadness
Often change to night our day.

Heaven is here, where misery lightened
  Of its heavy load is seen;
Where the face of sorrow brightened
  By the deed of love has been;

Where the bound, the poor, despairing,
  Are set free, supplied and blest;
Where, in others' labours sharing,
  We can find our surest rest;

Where we heed the voice of duty
  More than earthly crown or rod;
This is heaven – its peace, its beauty,
  Radiant with the smile of God.

*J. G. Adams**

322

Cromer L.M.

I LEARNED it in the meadow path,
  I learned it on the mountain stairs –
The best things any mortal hath
  Are those which every mortal shares.

The air we breathe, the sky, the breeze,
  The light without us and within,
Life with its unlocked treasuries,
  God's riches, are for all to win.

The grass is softer to my tread
  Because it rests unnumbered feet;
Sweeter to me the wild rose red,
  Because she makes the whole world sweet.

Wealth won by others' poverty –
  Not such be mine! let me be blest
Only in what they share with me,
  And what I share with all the rest.

And up the radiant peopled way
  That opens into worlds unknown
It will be life's delight to say,
  "Heaven is not heaven for me alone"

Lucy Larcom

323

Salzburg C.M.

O GOD of Bethel, by whose hand
Thy people still are fed;
Who through this earthly pilgrimage
Hast all our forebears led!

Our vows, our prayers, we now present
Before thy throne of grace;
God of our forebears, be the God
Of their succeeding race.

Through each perplexing path of life
Our wandering footsteps guide;
Give us each day our daily bread
And raiment fit provide.

O spread thy covering wings around
Till all our wanderings cease;
And at our Father's loved abode
Our souls arrive in peace.

Now with the humble voice of prayer
Thy mercy we implore;
Then with the grateful voice of praise
Thy goodness we'll adore.

*Philip Doddridge**

324

Marching 87.87.

THROUGH the night of doubt and sorrow,
Onward goes the pilgrim band,
Singing songs of expectation,
Marching to the promised land.

Clear before us through the darkness
Gleams and burns the guiding light;
Sister clasps the hand of brother,
Stepping fearless through the night.

One the light of God's own presence,
O'er his ransomed people shed,
Chasing far the gloom and terror,
Brightening all the path we tread;

One the object of our journey,
One the faith which never tires,
One the earnest looking forward,
One the hope our God inspires;

One the strain that lips of thousands
Lift as from the heart of one;
One the conflict, one the peril,
One the march in God begun;

One the gladness of rejoicing
On the far eternal shore,
Where the one Almighty Father
Reigns in love for evermore!

*B. S. Ingemann, trans. S. Baring-Gould**

325

Lux benigna/Sandon 10 4.10 4.10 10.

LEAD, kindly light! amid the encircling gloom,
Lead thou me on!
The night is dark, and I am far from home –
Lead thou me on!
Keep thou my feet: I do not ask to see
The distant scene – one step enough for me.

I was not ever thus, nor prayed that thou
Shouldst lead me on.
I loved to choose and see my path; but now –
Lead thou me on!
I loved the garish day; and, spite of fears,
Pride ruled my will: remember not past years!

So long thy power hath blessed me, sure it still
Will lead me on.
O'er moor and fen, o'er crag and torrent, till
The night is gone,
And, with the morn, those angel faces smile
Which I have loved long since, and lost awhile.

John Henry Newman

326

Cwm Rhondda 87.87.87.

GUIDE me, O thou great Jehovah,
Pilgrim through this barren land;
I am weak, but thou art mighty;
Hold me with thy powerful hand:
Bread of heaven,
Feed me now and evermore.

Open thou the crystal fountain,
Whence the healing stream shall flow;
Let the fiery, cloudy pillar
Lead me all my journey through:
Strong Deliverer,
Be thou still my strength and shield.

When I tread the verge of Jordan,
Bid my anxious fears subside;
Death of death, and hell's destruction,
Land me safe on Canaan's side:
Songs of praises
I will ever give to thee.

W. Williams, trans. P. Williams and others

327

Mannheim 87.87.87

LEAD us, heavenly Father, lead us
O'er the world's tempestuous sea;
Guard us, guide us, keep us, feed us,
For we have no help but thee;
Yet possessing every blessing
If our God our Father be.

Jesus, breathe forgiveness o'er us;
  All our weakness thou dost know,
Thou didst tread this earth before us,
  Thou didst feel its keenest woe;
Tempted, taunted, yet undaunted,
  Through the desert thou didst go.

Spirit of our God, descending,
  Fill our hearts with heavenly joy,
Love with every passion blending,
  Pleasure that can never cloy;
Thus provided, pardoned, guided,
  Nothing can our peace destroy.

*J. Edmeston**

328

St. Agnes 10 10.10 10.

LEAD us, O Father, in the paths of peace;
Without thy guiding hand we go astray,
And doubts appal, and sorrows still increase;
Lead us through Christ, the true and living Way.

Lead us, O Father, in the paths of truth;
Unhelped by thee, in error's maze we grope,
While passion stains and folly dims our youth,
And age comes on uncheered by faith and hope.

Lead us, O Father, in the paths of right;
Blindly we stumble when we walk alone,
Involved in shadows of a starless night:
Only with thee we journey safely on.

Lead us, O Father, to thy heavenly rest,
However rough and steep the path may be,
Through joy or sorrow, as thou deemest best,
Until our lives are perfected in thee.

*W. B. Burleigh**

329

Abbot's Leigh 87.87.D

COURAGE, friend, and do not stumble,
Though thy path be dark as night;
There's a star to guide the humble –
Trust in God, and do the right.
Let the road be rough and dreary,
And its end far out of sight,
Foot it bravely, strong or weary,
Trust in God, and do the right.

Perish policy and cunning,
Perish all that fears the light!
Whether losing, whether winning,
Trust in God, and do the right.
Some will hate thee, some will love thee,
Some will flatter, some will slight:
Lift thine eyes and look above thee,
Trust in God, and do the right.

Clouds and sunshine both await thee,
Noonday radiance, stormy night,
Yet through all he'll safely lead thee,
Trust in God, and do the right.
Simple rule, and safest guiding,
Inward peace, and inward light,
Star upon our path abiding –
Trust in God, and do the right.

*N. MacLeod**

330

St. James C.M.

SHINE on our souls, eternal God!
With rays of beauty shine;
O let thy favour crown our days,
And all their round be thine.

Did we not raise our hearts to thee,
Our hands might toil in vain;
Small joy success itself could give,
If thou thy love restrain.

With thee let every week begin;
With thee each day be spent;
For thee each fleeting hour improved,
Since each by thee is lent.

Thus cheer us through the desert road,
Till all our labours cease,
And heaven refresh our weary souls
With everlasting peace.

Philip Doddridge

331

Fulda *L.M.*

GRANT us thy light, that we may know
The wisdom thou alone canst give;
That truth may guide where'er we go,
And virtue bless where'er we live.

Grant us thy light, that we may see
Where error lurks in human lore,
And turn our doubting minds to thee,
And love thy simple word the more.

Grant us thy light, that we may learn
How dead is life from thee apart;
How sure is joy for all who turn
To thee an undivided heart.

Grant us thy light, in grief and pain,
To lift our burdened hearts above;
And count the very cross a gain,
And bless our Father's hidden love.

Grant us thy light, when, soon or late,
All earthly scenes shall pass away,
In thee to find the open gate
To deathless home and endless day.

L. Tuttiett

332

Penlan 76.76.D.

In heavenly love abiding,
No change my heart shall fear;
And safe is such confiding,
For nothing changes here.
The storm may roar outside me,
My heart may low be laid;
But God is round about me,
And can I be dismayed?

Wherever he may guide me,
No want shall turn me back;
My Shepherd is beside me,
And nothing can I lack.
His wisdom ever waketh,
His sight is never dim;
He knows the way he taketh,
And I will walk with him.

Green pastures are before me,
Which yet I have not seen;
Bright skies will soon be o'er me
Where darkest clouds have been.
My hope I cannot measure,
My path in life is free:
The Lord hath all my treasure,
And he will walk with me.

*Anna L. Waring**

333

Sharon 87.87.

When the light of day is waning,
When the night is dark and drear,
God of love, in stillness reigning,
Teach me to believe thee near.

When my heart is faint and drooping,
When my faith is weak and cold,
Kindly to my weakness stooping,
Draw me upwards as of old.

Nearer to the peace unbroken,
  Nearer to the changeless calm,
All my wish a prayer unspoken,
  All my life a silent psalm.

Teach me to abide in patience
  All the little storms of time,
Making every day's temptations
  Steps for faltering feet to climb.

Let me find thee in my sorrow,
  Nor forget thee in my joy;
And from thee my sunshine borrow,
  And by thee my gloom destroy.

God of day, the dark dispelling,
  Guide, Redeemer, Father, Friend,
God of Love, in stillness dwelling,
  Lead me to my journey's end

E. M. Geldart

334

Nativity C.M.

WALK in the light, so shalt thou know
  That fellowship of love
His Spirit only can bestow,
  Who reigns in light above.

Walk in the light, and thou shalt find
  Thy heart made truly his,
Who dwells in cloudless light enshrined,
  In whom no darkness is.

Walk in the light, and thou shalt own
  Thy darkness passed away,
Because that light hath on thee shone
  In which is perfect day.

Walk in the light, and thine shall be
  A path, though thorny, bright;
For God, by grace, shall dwell in thee,
  And God himself is Light.

B. Barton

335

Beatitudo C.M.

SPIRIT of Faith! be thou my guide;
O clasp my hand in thine
And never let me quit thy side;
Thy comforts are divine.

Pride scorns thee for thy lowly mien;
But who like thee can rise
So high above this sordid scene,
So near the holy skies?

Gentle thine eye, and soft thy voice,
But wondrous is thy might,
To make the wretched soul rejoice,
To give the simple light.

And still to all who seek thy way
The wondrous power is given,
That while their footsteps press the clay,
Their souls ascend to heaven.

Through pain and death I can rejoice
If but thy strength be mine;
Earth hath no music like thy voice,
Life owns no joy like thine.

Spirit of Faith! I'll go with thee,
Thou, if I hold thee fast,
Wilt guide, defend and strengthen me,
And bear me home at last.

Anne Bronte

336

Wiltshire C.M.

THROUGH all the winding ways of life,
In shadow and in shine,
Beyond all craving and all strife,
O Lord, preserve us thine.

Thine on this earth, and thine above,
For ever, all thine own:
Thee, O our long-enduring Love,
We need, and thee alone.

By thee we love, and by thee live,
Our origin, our goal;
Thyself, thy full perfection give
To keep and rule the soul.

Not only for ourselves we pray –
That prayer no fruit can bear;
We are unhappy on thy way
Without each other near.

Dear Father of the human heart,
The whole wide world atone;
What thou hast been to us, impart
To all; make all thine own.

*S. A. Brooke**

337

Amazing Grace C.M.

AMAZING grace – such love profound
That saves and strengthens me!
I once was lost, but now am found,
Was blind, but now I see.

Through many dangers, toils and snares
I have already come;
God's grace has brought me safe thus far,
And he will lead me home.

The Lord has promised good to me –
His word my hope secures;
He will my shield and portion be
As long as life endures.

And, when this heart and flesh shall fail
And mortal life shall cease,
I shall possess within the veil
A life of joy and peace.

*John Newton**

338

Channel of Peace *Irregular*

MAKE me a channel of your peace.
Where there is hatred, let me bring your love;
Where there is injury, your pardon, Lord;
And where there's doubt, true faith in you:

O Master, grant that I may never seek
So much to be consoled as to console;
To be understood as to understand;
To be loved, as to love with all my soul.

Make me a channel of your peace.
Where there's despair in life, let me bring hope;
Where there is darkness, only light;
And where there's sadness, ever joy:

O Master, grant that I may never seek
So much to be consoled as to console;
To be understood as to understand;
To be loved, as to love with all my soul.

Make me a channel of your peace.
It is in pardoning that we are pardoned,
In giving to all that we receive,
And in dying that we're born to eternal life.

based on a traditional prayer

TRUST IN GOD

339

St. Anne C.M.

O GOD, our help in ages past,
Our hope for years to come,
Our shelter from the stormy blast,
And our eternal home!

Beneath the shadow of thy throne
Thy saints have dwelt secure;
Sufficient is thine arm alone,
And our defence is sure.

Before the hills in order stood,
  Or earth received her frame,
From everlasting thou art God,
  To endless years the same.

A thousand ages in thy sight
  Are like an evening gone,
Short as the watch that ends the night
  Before the rising sun.

Time, like an ever-rolling stream,
  Bears all of us away;
We fly forgotten, as a dream
  Dies at the opening day.

O God our help in ages past,
  Our hope for years to come,
Be thou our guard while troubles last,
  And our eternal home.

*Isaac Watts**

340

Ein' feste Burg *87.87.66.667.*

A MIGHTY fortress is our God,
  A bulwark never failing;
Our helper he, amid the flood
  Of mortal ills prevailing.
For still our ancient foe
Doth seek to work us woe;
His craft and power are great,
And, armed with cruel hate,
  On earth is not his equal.

With force of arms we nothing can,
  Full soon were we down-ridden;
But for us fights the proper Man,
  Whom God himself hath bidden.
Ask ye: Who is this same?
Christ Jesus is his name,
The Lord Sabaoth's Son;
He, and no other one,
  Shall conquer in the battle.

God's word above all earthly powers –
  No thanks to them – abideth;
The Spirit and the gifts are ours,
  Through him who with us sideth.
Let goods and kindred go,
This mortal life also;
The body they may kill;
God's truth abideth still;
  His kingdom is for ever.

Martin Luther, trans. F. H. Hedge and T. Carlyle

341

Llangloffan 76.76.D.

GOD is my strong salvation,
  What foe have I to fear?
In darkness and temptation,
  My light, my help is near:
Though hosts encamp around me,
  Firm to the fight I stand;
What terror can confound me,
  With God at my right hand?

Place on the Lord reliance,
  My soul, with courage wait;
His truth be thine affiance,
  When faint and desolate;
His might thy heart shall strengthen,
  His love thy joy increase;
Mercy thy days shall lengthen;
  The Lord will give thee peace.

J. Montgomery

342

Michael 87.87.337.

ALL my hope on God is founded;
He doth still my trust renew,
Me through change and chance he guideth,
Only good and only true.
God unknown,
He alone
Calls my heart to be his own.

Human pride and earthly glory,
Sword and crown betray our trust:
What with care and toil we fashion,
Tower and temple fall to dust,
But God's power,
Hour by hour,
Is my temple and my tower.

God's great goodness aye endureth,
Deep his wisdom passing thought:
Splendour, light and life attend him,
Beauty springeth out of nought.
Evermore
From his store
New-born worlds rise and adore.

Daily doth th'Almighty Giver
Bounteous gifts on us bestow.
His desire our soul delighteth,
Pleasure leads us where we go.
Love doth stand
At his hand;
Joy doth wait on his command.

Still from us to God eternal
Sacrifice of praise be done,
High above all praises praising
For the gift of Christ his Son.
Christ doth call
One and all:
Ye who follow shall not fall.

R. Bridges, after J. Neander*

343

London New C.M.

GOD moves in a mysterious way
His wonders to perform;
He plants his footsteps in the sea,
And rides upon the storm.

Deep in unfathomable mines
Of never-failing skill
He treasures up his bright designs,
And works his sovereign will.

Ye fearful saints, fresh courage take;
The clouds ye so much dread
Are big with mercy, and shall break
In blessings on your head.

Judge not the Lord by feeble sense,
But trust him for his grace;
Behind a frowning providence
He hides a smiling face.

His purposes will ripen fast,
Unfolding every hour;
The bud may have a bitter taste,
But sweet will be the flower.

Blind unbelief is sure to err,
And scan his work in vain;
God is his own interpreter,
And he will make it plain.

William Cowper

344

Luther's Hymn 87.87.887.

LORD, thou hast been our dwelling-place
In every generation;
Thy people still have known thy grace,
And blessed thy consolation;
Through every age thou heardst our cry;
Through every age we found thee nigh,
Our strength and our salvation.

Our cleaving sins we oft have wept,
  And oft thy patience provèd;
But still thy faith we fast have kept,
  Thy name we still have lovèd:
And thou hast kept and loved us well,
Hast granted us in thee to dwell,
  Unshaken, unremovèd.

Lord nothing from thine arms of love
  Shall thine own people sever,
Our Helper never will remove,
  Our God will fail us never:
Thy people, Lord, have dwelt in thee,
Our dwelling-place thou still wilt be
  For ever and for ever.

T. H. Gill

345

Colchester 88.88.88.

NOT only in the sunshine, Lord,
  When life is glad and sings aloud,
With all about us in accord,
  But we would praise thee in the cloud:
Then let us lift our gaze above,
And thank thee for the heart of love.

When in the misty dark we stand
  And strain our aching eyes to see;
When without help from other hand
  We lift our weary arms to thee:
Then let us feel our firmest stay –
Thy love that cannot pass away.

Where'er we go, despite our fear,
  Still may we know, beneath our doubt,
The sense that thou art ever near,
  Thy loving presence round about:
No more we wander in despair,
The eternal heart of love is there.

T. E. Harvey

346

Caterham C.M.

ALL as God wills! who wisely heeds
To give or to withhold,
And knoweth more of all my needs
Than all my prayers have told.

Enough that blessings undeserved
Have marked my erring track;
That wheresoe'er my feet have swerved,
His chastening turned me back;

That more and more a Providence
Of love is understood,
Making the springs of time and sense
Sweet with eternal good;

That all the jarring notes of life
Seem blending in a psalm,
And all the angles of its strife
Slow rounding into calm;

That death seems but a covered way,
Which opens into light,
Wherein no blinded child can stray
Beyond the Father's sight.

And so the shadows fall apart,
And so the west winds play;
And all the windows of my heart
I open to the day!

J. G. Whittier

347

St. Cecilia 66.66.

THY way, not mine, O Lord,
However dark it be!
Lead me by thine own hand;
Choose out the path for me.

Smooth let it be, or rough,
It will be still the best;
Winding or straight, it leads
Right onward to thy rest.

I dare not choose my lot;
I would not, if I might:
Choose thou for me, my God;
So shall I walk aright.

Choose thou for me my friends,
My sickness or my health;
Choose thou my cares for me,
My poverty or wealth.

Not mine, not mine, the choice,
In things or great or small:
Be thou my guide, my strength,
My wisdom, and my all.

H. Bonar

348

St. Francis *C.M.*

THY way is in the deep, O Lord!
E'en there we'll go with thee:
We'll meet the tempest at thy word,
And walk upon the sea!

Poor tremblers at his rougher wind,
Why do we doubt him so?
Who gives the storm a path, will find
The way our feet shall go.

A moment may his hand be lost –
Dread moment of delay!
We cry, "Lord! help the tempest-tossed",
And safe we're borne away.

The Lord yields nothing to our fears,
And flies from selfish care;
But comes himself, where'er he hears
The voice of loving prayer.

O happy soul of faith divine,
  Thy victory how sure!
The love that kindles joy is thine,
  The patience to endure.

Come, Lord of peace! our griefs dispel
  And wipe our tears away:
'Tis thine to order all things well,
  And ours to bless the sway.

*James Martineau**

349

Melita 88.88.88

ETERNAL Father, strong to save,
Whose arm doth bind the restless wave,
Who bidd'st the mighty ocean deep
Its own appointed limits keep:
  O hear us when we cry to thee
  For those in peril on the sea.

O Jesus, whose rebuking word
The winds and waves submissive heard,
Who walkedst on the foaming deep,
And calm amid its rage didst sleep:

O sacred Spirit, who didst brood
Upon the chaos dark and rude,
Who bad'st its angry tumult cease.
And gavest light and life and peace:

Almighty God of love and power,
Our brethren shield in danger's hour;
From rock and tempest, fire and foe,
Protect them wheresoe'er they go:
  And ever let there rise to thee
  Glad hymns of praise from land and sea.

*W. Whiting**

350

Harts 77.77.

MANY things in life there are
Past our understanding far,
And the humblest flower that grows
Hides a secret no one knows.

All unread by outer sense
Lies the soul's experience;
Mysteries around us rise,
We, the deeper mysteries!

While we may so little scan
Of thy vast creation's plan,
Teach us, O our God, to be
Humble in our walk with thee!

May we trust, through ill and good,
Thine unchanging Fatherhood,
And our highest wisdom find
In the reverent heart and mind!

Clearer vision shall be ours,
Larger wisdom, ampler powers,
And the meaning yet appear
Of what passes knowledge here.

*F. L. Hosmer**

351

New Malden/Rhuddlan 87.87.87

WHEN our confidence is shaken
In beliefs we thought secure;
When the spirit in its sickness
Seeks but cannot find a cure:
God is active in the tensions
Of a faith not yet mature.

Solar systems, void of meaning,
Freeze the spirit into stone;
Always our researches lead us
To the ultimate Unknown:
Faith must die, or come full circle
To its source in God alone.

In the discipline of praying,
  When it's hardest to believe;
In the drudgery of caring,
  When it's not enough to grieve:
Faith, maturing, learns acceptance
  Of the insights we receive.

God is love; and he redeems us
  In the Christ we crucify:
This is God's eternal answer
  To the world's eternal why;
May we in this faith maturing
  Be content to live and die!

F. Pratt Green

352

Aberystwyth 77.77.D.

FATHER, refuge of my soul,
  Let me to thy shelter fly:
While the nearer waters roll,
While the tempest still is high:
Hide me, O my Father, hide,
Till the storm of life be past:
Safe into the haven guide;
O receive my soul at last!

Other refuge have I none;
Hangs my helpless soul on thee:
Leave, O leave me not alone;
Still support and comfort me.
All my trust on thee is stayed:
All my help from thee I bring;
Cover my defenceless head
With the shadow of thy wing.

Plenteous grace with thee is found;
Cleanse me, Lord, from every sin:
Let the healing streams abound;
Make and keep me pure within.

Thou of life the fountain art;
Freely let me take of thee:
Spring thou up within my heart;
Rise to all eternity.

*Charles Wesley**

353

Love Unknown 66.66.88.

OFT when of God we ask
For fuller, happier life,
He sets us some new task,
Involving care and strife:
Is this the boon for which we sought?
Has prayer new trouble on us brought?

This indeed the boon,
Though strange to us it seems;
We pierce the rock, and soon
The blessing on us streams:
For when we are the most athirst,
Then the clear waters on us burst.

We toil as in a field
Wherein, to us unknown,
A treasure lies concealed,
Which may be all our own:
And shall we of the toil complain,
That speedily will bring such gain?

We dig the wells of life,
And God the water gives;
We win our way by strife,
Then he within us lives:
And only war could make us meet
For peace so sacred and complete.

*T. T. Lynch**

354

Walsall C.M.

I SEE the wrong that round me lies,
I feel the guilt within;
I hear, with groan and travail-cries,
The world confess its sin:

Yet, in the maddening maze of things,
  And tossed by storm and flood,
To one fixed trust my spirit clings:
  I know that God is good.

Not mine to look where cherubim
  And seraphs may not see,
But nothing can be good in him
  Which evil is in me.

The wrong that pains my soul below
  I dare not throne above:
I know not of his hate – I know
  His goodness and his love!

I dimly guess from blessings known
  Of greater out of sight,
And, with the chastened Psalmist, own
  His judgements too are right.

J. G. Whittier

355

Franconia S.M.

BLEST be thy love, dear Lord,
  That taught us this wise way,
Only to love thee for thyself,
  And for that love obey.

O thou, our soul's chief hope,
  We to thy mercy fly:
Where'er we are, thou canst protect,
  Whate'er we need, supply.

Whether we sleep or wake,
  To thee we both resign;
By night we see, as well as day,
  If thy light on us shine.

Whether we live or die,
  Both we submit to thee;
In death we live, as well as life,
  If thine in death we be.

*J. Austin**

356

Meirionydd/Missionary 76.76. D.

SOMETIMES a light surprises
  The Christian while he sings;
It is the Lord, who rises
  With healing in his wings:
When comforts are declining,
  He grants the soul again
A season of clear shining,
  To cheer it after rain.

In holy contemplation
  We firmly then pursue
The theme of God's salvation,
  And find it ever new;
Set free from present sorrow,
  We cheerfully can say,
E'en let the unknown morrow
  Bring with it what it may.

It can bring with it nothing
  But he will bear us through;
Who gives the lilies clothing
  Will clothe his people too:
Beneath the spreading heavens
  No creature but is fed;
And he who feeds the ravens
  Will give his children bread.

Though vine, nor fig-tree neither,
  Its wonted fruit should bear;
Though all the field should wither,
  Nor flocks, nor herds be there,
Yet God the same abiding,
  His praise shall tune my voice;
For while in him confiding
  I cannot but rejoice.

*William Cowper**

357

St. Matthew C.M.D.

O THOU who art of all that is
Beginning both and end,
We follow thee through unknown paths,
Since all to thee must tend:
Thy judgements are a mighty deep
Beyond all fathom-line;
Our wisdom is the childlike heart,
Our strength, to trust in thine.

We bless thee for the skies above,
And for the earth beneath,
For hopes that blossom here below
And wither not with death;
But most we bless thee for thyself,
O heavenly Light within,
Whose dayspring in our hearts dispels
The darkness of our sin.

Be thou in joy our deeper joy,
Our comfort when distressed,
Be thou by day our strength for toil,
And thou by night our rest.
And when these earthly dwellings fail
And time's last hour is come,
Be thou, O God, our dwelling-place
And our eternal home!

F. L. Hosmer

358

Palmyra 86.86.88.

I LOOK to thee in every need,
And never look in vain;
I feel thy strong and tender love,
And all is well again;
The thought of thee is mightier far
Than sin and pain and sorrow are.

Discouraged in the work of life,
  Disheartened by its load,
Shamed by its failures or its fears,
  I sink beside the road –
But let me only think of thee,
And then new heart springs up in me.

Thy calmness bends serene above,
  My restlessness to still;
Around me flows thy quickening life,
  To nerve my faltering will;
Thy presence fills my solitude;
Thy providence turns all to good.

Embosomed deep in thy dear love,
  Held in thy law, I stand;
Thy hand in all things I behold,
  And all things in thy hand;
Thou leadest me by unsought ways,
And turn'st my mourning into praise.

S. Longfellow

359

Nativity C.M.

ONE that is down needs fear no fall,
  One that is low no pride;
One that is humble ever shall
  Have God to be the guide.

I am content with what I have,
  Little be it or much;
And, Lord, contentment still I crave
  Because thou savest such.

Fulness to such a burden is
  That go on pilgrimage;
Here little, and hereafter bliss
  Is best from age to age.

*John Bunyan**

360

Horbury 64.64.664.

NEARER, my God, to thee,
Nearer to thee!
E'en though it be a cross
That raiseth me;
Still all my song shall be –
Nearer, my God, to thee,
Nearer to thee.

Though, like the wanderer,
The sun gone down,
Darkness be over me,
My rest a stone;
Yet in my dreams I'd be
Nearer, my God, to thee,
Nearer to thee.

There let the way appear,
Steps unto heaven;
All that thou sendest me
In mercy given;
Angels to beckon me
Nearer, my God to thee,
Nearer to thee.

Then with my waking thoughts
Bright with thy praise,
Out of my stony griefs
Bethel I'll raise;
So by my woes to be
Nearer, my God, to thee,
Nearer to thee.

Or if on joyful wing
Cleaving the sky,
Sun, moon, and stars forgot,
Upward I fly;
Still all my song shall be –
Nearer, my God, to thee,
Nearer to thee.

Sarah F. Adams

361

Kingsland 66.66.

MY spirit longs for thee
Within my troubled breast,
Though I unworthy be
Of so divine a guest:

Of so divine a guest
Unworthy though I be,
Yet has my heart no rest,
Unless it come from thee:

Unless it come from thee,
In vain I look around:
In all that I can see
No rest is to be found:

No rest is to be found,
But in thy blessèd love:
O let my wish be crowned,
And send it from above!

J. Byrom

362

Ratisbon 77.77.77.

THOU, whose glory fills the skies,
Thou, the true, the only Light,
Sun of Righteousness, arise,
Triumph o'er the shades of night;
Dayspring from on high, be near;
Daystar, in my heart appear.

Dark and cheerless is the morn
Unaccompanied by thee;
Joyless is the day's return,
Till thy mercy's beams I see;
Till thou inward light impart,
Glad my eyes, and warm my heart.

Visit, then, this soul of mine;
Pierce the gloom of sin and grief;
Fill me, Radiancy divine;
Scatter all my unbelief;
More and more thyself display,
Shining to the perfect day.

*Charles Wesley**

363

Goshen 65.65.D.

In life's earnest morning,
When our hope was high,
Came thy voice in summons,
Not to be put by:
Nor in toil nor sorrow,
Weakness nor dismay,
Need we ever falter –
Art not thou our stay?

Teach us, Lord, thy wisdom,
Seeking human skill;
May the mind be humbled
As we know thy will;
Let the larger vision
Bring the childlike heart,
And our deeper knowledge
Holier zeal impart.

Should our faith be palsied
By the touch of doubt,
Should our hearts grow empty,
Faithless, undevout,
Lord, in mercy lead us
To our springs in thee,
Where are healing waters
Plentiful and free.

Should thy face be clouded
To our spirits' sight,
Speak through human kindness,
Shine through Nature's light,
In the face of loved ones,
Or the ties of home –
Only, gracious Father,
To thy children come.

Save us, Lord, from seeking
Earth's unhallowed goals;
May our life-long passion
Be the love of souls;
Let us live and labour,
Father, in thy sight,
Through the grace of Jesus,
By the Spirit's might.

*E. S. Oakley**

364

St. Agnes Durham C.M.

My heart is resting, O my God!
I will give thanks and sing:
My heart is at the secret source
Of every precious thing.

I thirst for springs of heavenly life,
And here all day they rise:
I seek the treasure of thy love,
And close at hand it lies.

Glory to thee for strength withheld,
For want and weakness known,
The fear that sends me to thy breast
For what is most mine own.

Mine be the reverent listening love
That waits all day on thee;
The service of a watchful heart
Which no one else can see;

The faith that, in a hidden way,
No other eye may know,
Finds all its daily work prepared,
And loves to have it so.

My heart is resting, O my God!
My heart is in thy care;
I hear the voice of joy and praise
Resounding everywhere.

Anna L. Waring

365

Beatitudo C.M.

PRAYER is the soul's sincere desire,
Uttered or unexpressed,
The motion of a hidden fire
That trembles in the breast.

Prayer is the burden of a sigh,
The falling of a tear,
The upward glancing of an eye
When none but God is near.

Prayer is the simplest form of speech
That infant lips can try;
Prayer the sublimest strains that reach
The majesty on high.

Prayer is the contrite sinner's voice
Returning from his ways,
While angels in their songs rejoice,
And cry: "Behold, he prays!"

Prayer is the Christian's vital breath,
The Christian's native air,
Our watchword at the gates of death;
We enter heaven with prayer.

O thou by whom we come to God,
The Life, the Truth, the Way!
The path of prayer thyself hast trod:
Lord, teach us how to pray!

J. Montgomery

366

Beatitudo C.M.

WE do not seek a shallow faith,
A God to keep us free
From trial and error, harm and death,
Wherever we may be.

For none can live and not grow old,
Nor love and not risk loss:
Though life bring raptures manifold,
Each one must bear some cross.

When future days seem but a mass
Of menace more than hope,
We pray not for the cup to pass,
But strength that we may cope.

God grant us faith that when some ill
Unwonted comes our way,
Deep in our hearts, thy Spirit will
Give power to win the day.

And if from fear of pain or strife,
Calm peace we cannot win,
Then give us faith to trust thy Life
Invincible within.

Sydney H. Knight

367

Finnart L.M.

THOU Power and Peace, in whom we find
All holiest strength, all purest love,
The rushing of the mighty wind,
The brooding of the gentle dove!

For ever lend thy sovereign aid,
And urge us on, and keep us thine;
Nor leave the hearts which thou hast made
Fit temples of thy grace divine.

Nor let us quench thy saving light;
But still with softest breathings stir
Our wayward souls, and lead us right,
O God of Peace, the Comforter!

Cecil Frances Alexander

368

Morning Prayer 65.65.D.

PURER yet and purer
  I would be in mind,
Dearer yet and dearer
  Every duty find;
Hoping still, and trusting
  God without a fear,
Patiently believing
  He will make all clear.

Calmer yet and calmer
  In the hours of pain,
Surer yet and surer
  Peace at last to gain;
Suffering still and doing,
  To his will resigned,
And to God subduing
  Heart and will and mind.

Higher yet and higher
  Out of clouds and night,
Nearer yet and nearer
  Rising to the light –
Light serene and holy,
  Where my soul may rest,
Purified and lowly,
  Sanctified and blest.

Anon.

369

Samuel 66.66.88.

HUSHED was the evening hymn,
The Temple courts were dark;
The lamp was burning dim
Before the sacred ark;
When suddenly a voice divine
Rang through the silence of the shrine.

The old man, meek and mild,
The priest of Israel, slept;
His watch the Temple child,
The little Levite kept;
And what from Eli's sense was sealed
The Lord to Hannah's son revealed.

O give me Samuel's ear,
The open ear, O Lord,
Alive and quick to hear
Each whisper of thy word:
Like him to answer at thy call,
And to obey thee first of all.

O give me Samuel's heart,
A lowly heart that waits,
Where in thy house thou art,
Or watches at thy gates
By day and night – a heart that still
Moves at the breathing of thy will.

O give me Samuel's mind,
A firm unmurmuring faith,
Obedient and resigned
To thee in life and death;
That I may read with childlike eyes
Truths that are hidden from the wise.

*J. D. Burns**

370

Rosslyn 77.77.

LORD, forgive me, day by day,
Debts I cannot hope to pay;
Duties I have left undone,
Evils I have failed to shun:

Trespasses in word and thought;
Deeds from evil motive wrought;
Cold ingratitude, distrust;
Thoughts unhallowed or unjust.

Pardon, Lord; and are there those
Who my debtors are, or foes?
I, who by forgiveness live,
Here their trespasses forgive.

Much forgiven, may I learn
Love for hatred to return;
Then assured my heart shall be,
Thou, my God, hast pardoned me.

J. Conder

371

Down Ampney 66.11.D.

COME down, O Love divine,
Seek thou this soul of mine,
And visit it with thine own ardour glowing;
O Comforter, draw near,
Within my heart appear,
And kindle it, thy holy flame bestowing.

O let it freely burn,
Till earthly passions turn
To dust and ashes in its heat consuming;
And let thy glorious light
Shine ever on my sight,
And clothe me round, the while my path illuming.

Let holy charity
Mine outward vesture be,
And lowliness possess mine inmost being;
True lowliness of heart,
Which takes the humbler part,
And thus repents, its own shortcomings seeing.

And so the yearning strong,
With which the soul will long,
Shall far outpass the power of human telling;
For none can guess its grace,
Till he become the place
Wherein the Holy Spirit makes his dwelling.

*Bianco da Siena, trans. R. F. Littledale**

372

St. George S.M.

STILL with thee, O my God,
I would desire to be:
By day, by night, at home, abroad,
I would be still with thee.

With thee, amid the crowd
That throngs the busy mart,
To hear thy voice, 'mid clamour loud,
Speak softly to my heart;

With thee, when day is done,
And evening calms the mind:
The setting as the rising sun
With thee my heart would find;

With thee, when darkness brings
The signal of repose;
Calm in the shadow of thy wings
Mine eyelids I would close.

With thee, in thee, by faith
Abiding would I be;
By day, by night, in life, in death
I would be still with thee.

J. D. Burns

373

Stella 88.88.88.

THOU hidden love of God, whose height,
Whose depth unfathomed, no one knows!
I see from far thy beauteous light,
Inly I sigh for thy repose;
Then shall my heart from care be free,
When it hath found repose in thee.

Father, thy sovereign aid impart,
To save me from low-thoughted care!
Chase this self-will through all my heart,
Through all its latent mazes there:
Make me thy duteous child, that I
Ceaseless may "Abba, Father" cry.

Each moment draw from earth away
My heart that lowly waits thy call!
Speak to my inmost soul and say,
"I am thy life, thy God, thy all!"
Thy love to know, thy voice to hear,
Thy power to feel, be all my prayer.

*G. Tersteegen, trans. John Wesley**

374

St. Ethelwald S.M.

AT first I prayed for Light;
Could I but see the way,
How gladly, swiftly would I walk
To everlasting day!

And next I prayed for Strength,
That I might tread the road
With firm, unfaltering feet, and win
The heaven's serene abode.

And then I asked for Faith;
Could I but trust my God,
I'd live enfolded in his peace,
Though foes were all abroad.

But now I pray for Love,
Deep love to God, to all;
A living love that will not fail,
However far we fall;

And Light and Strength and Faith
Are opening everywhere!
God only waited for me till
I prayed the larger prayer.

*Edna D. Cheney**

375

White Ladies Aston 77.77.

FATHER, we look up to thee!
Let us in thy love agree:
Thou, who art the God of peace,
Bid contention ever cease.

Make us of one heart and mind,
Courteous, merciful, and kind;
Lowly, meek in thought and word,
Ne'er by fretful passion stirred.

Let us for each other care,
Each the other's burden bear;
Ready, when reviled, to bless;
Studious of the law of peace.

Father, all our souls inspire;
Fill us with love's sacred fire!
Guided by that blessèd light,
Order all our steps aright.

Free from anger, free from pride,
Let us thus in thee abide;
All the depth of love express,
All the height of holiness.

Charles Wesley and others

376

The Call 77.77.

COME, my way, my truth, my life:
Such a way as gives us breath,
Such a truth as ends all strife,
Such a life as killeth death.

Come, my light, my feast, my strength:
Such a light as shows a feast,
Such a feast as mends in length,
Such a strength as makes his guest.

Come, my joy, my love, my heart:
Such a joy as none can move,
Such a love as none can part,
Such a heart as joys in love.

George Herbert

377

Manchester College 10 4.10 4.

DIVINITY is round us – never gone
From earth or star,
From life or death, from good or even wrong –
In all we are.

Seek not for God in only noblest deeds –
Those seldom done:
For God's life throbs in all our anguished needs
Beneath the sun.

We yearn for God in a perfected one
By signs foretold –
While in mistakes and virtues just begun
God's ways unfold.

Wait not at last in truth and love made whole
Your God to see;
In every timid, false, or angered soul
There's love to free.

Then wake, O Soul, respect yourself today;
Create your part;
And look to find your life and truth and way
With honest art.

Sophia Lyon Fahs

CLOSE OF LIFE AND BEYOND

378 *Eventide 10 10. 10 10.*

ABIDE with me; fast falls the eventide;
The darkness deepens; Lord, with me abide;
When other helpers fail, and comforts flee,
Help of the helpless, O abide with me.

Swift to its close ebbs out life's little day;
Earth's joys grow dim, its glories pass away;
Change and decay in all around I see;
O thou who changest not, abide with me!

I need thy presence every passing hour;
What but thy grace can foil the tempter's power?
Who like thyself my guide and stay can be?
Through cloud and sunshine, O abide with me.

I fear no foe, with thee at hand to bless;
Ills have no weight, and tears no bitterness;
Where is death's sting? Where, grave, thy victory?
I triumph still, if thou abide with me.

Hold thou thy cross before my closing eyes;
Shine through the gloom, and point me to the skies;
Heaven's morning breaks, and earth's vain shadows flee;
In life, in death, O Lord, abide with me!

H. F. Lyte

379

St. Marguerite C.M.

I CANNOT think of them as dead
  Who walk with me no more:
Along the path of life I tread
  They have but gone before.

The Father's house is mansioned fair
  Beyond my vision dim;
All souls are his and, here or there,
  Are living unto him.

And still their silent ministry
  Within my heart hath place,
As when on earth they walked with me,
  And met me face to face.

Their lives are made for ever mine;
  What they to me have been
Hath left henceforth its seal and sign
  Engraven deep within.

Mine are they by an ownership
  Nor time nor death can free;
For God hath given to Love to keep
  Its own eternally.

F. L. Hosmer

380

Horsley C.M.

NO longer forward or behind
  I look in hope or fear,
But, grateful, take the good I find,
  God's blessing now and here.

I know not what the future hath
  Of marvel or surprise,
Assured alone that life and death
  His mercy underlies.

And if my heart and flesh are weak
To bear an untried pain,
The bruisèd reed he will not break,
But strengthen and sustain.

And so beside the Silent Sea
I wait the muffled oar;
No harm from him can come to me
On ocean or on shore.

I know not where his islands lift
Their fronded palms in air;
I only know I cannot drift
Beyond his love and care.

J. G. Whittier

381

St. Matthias 88.88.88.

GOD of the living, in whose eyes
Unveiled thy whole creation lies!
All souls are thine; we must not say
That those are dead who pass away;
From this our world of sense set free,
We know them living unto thee.

Released from earthly toil and strife,
With thee is hidden still their life;
Thine are their thoughts, their works, their powers,
All thine, and yet most truly ours;
For well we know, where'er they be,
Our dead are living unto thee.

Not spilt like water on the ground,
Not wrapped in dreamless sleep profound,
Not wandering in unknown despair
Beyond thy voice, thine arm, thy care;
Not left to lie like fallen tree;
Not dead, but living unto thee.

O Breather into us of breath,
O Holder of the keys of death,
O Giver of the life within,
Save us from death, the death of sin;
That body, soul, and spirit be
For ever living unto thee.

*J. Ellerton**

382

Vulpius 888. with Alleluias

O LORD of Life, where'er they be,
Safe in thine own eternity,
Our dead are living unto thee.
Alleluia!

All souls are thine, and, here or there,
They rest within thy sheltering care;
One Providence alike they share.
Alleluia!

Thy word is true, thy ways are just;
Above the requiem, "Dust to dust,"
Shall rise our psalm of grateful trust.
Alleluia!

Oh, happy they in God who rest,
No more by fear and doubt oppressed;
Living or dying they are blest.
Alleluia!

F. L. Hosmer

383

Finlandia 11 10. 11 10. 11 10.

BE still, my soul: the Lord is on thy side;
Bear patiently the cross of grief or pain;
Leave to thy God to order and provide;
In every change he faithful will remain.
Be still, my soul: thy best, thy heavenly Friend
Through thorny ways leads to a joyful end.

Be still, my soul: thy God doth undertake
To guide the future as he has the past.
Thy hope, thy confidence let nothing shake;
All now mysterious shall be bright at last.
Be still, my soul: the waves and winds still know
His voice who ruled them while he dwelt below.

Be still, my soul: when dearest friends depart,
And all is darkened in the vale of tears,
Then shalt thou better know his love, his heart,
Who comes to soothe thy sorrow and thy fears.
Be still, my soul: our Father can repay,
From his own fullness, all he takes away.

Be still, my soul: the hour is hastening on
When we shall be forever with the Lord,
When disappointment, grief, and fear are gone,
Sorrow forgot, love's purest joys restored.
Be still, my soul: when change and tears are past,
All safe and blessèd we shall meet at last.

Katharina von Schlegel,
*trans. Jane Laurie Borthwick**

384

Ewing 76.76.D.

JERUSALEM the golden
With milk and honey blest,
Within thy contemplation
Are love, and life, and rest.
I know not, O, I know not
What joys await us there,
What radiancy of glory,
What bliss beyond compare.

They stand, those walls of Sion,
All jubilant with song,
And bright with many an angel,
And all the martyr throng;

And he whom now we trust in
Shall then be seen and known;
For God shall make his children
In perfectness his own.

O sweet and blessèd country,
That eager hearts expect;
Far, far belovèd country,
With holiness bedecked;
Thy children quickly waken,
Thy glories soon array;
Soon come, immortal conquest,
Soon dawn, eternal day.

J. M. Neale and S. A. Brooke, from St. Bernard

SPECIAL OCCASIONS

ORDINATION, INDUCTION, CHURCH DEDICATION

385 *London New* C.M.

O NOT to one, but all, our God,
Grant ordination free,
To heights of life as yet untrod,
And nobler ministry;

To tenderer words, to braver deeds,
To wills set fast in right,
To heart-beats rhymed to other's needs,
To love and life and light.

Ordain in all the seeker's mind
Of eager, trusting youth,
That hurries forth each morn to find
New manna-falls of truth.

Ordain the prophet-heart that takes
Lone sides with outcast worth;
Ordain the helping hand that makes
A dawn of heaven on earth.

*W. C. Gannett**

386

Warrington L.M.

GOD of our forebears hear our prayer:
Thy holy throne is everywhere;
Thine arm upheld thy saints of old,
And still is strong to guard thy fold.

Our forebears loved to hear thy word,
Ere freedom's sacred voice was heard;
And faithful kept, from age to age,
The truth, our noblest heritage.

Not as of old, with silent fear,
We raise our home and altar here;
Ours is the brighter, fairer day
Of Reason's light and Freedom's way.

Father, give thou thy blessing here,
Since to thy name this house we rear,
That ages yet unborn may share
The trust committed to our care.

Here let a church devout and free
Arise, devoted, Lord, to thee;
Our faith divine, our worship pure,
Our work abiding, firm, and sure.

*J. P. Hopps**

387

Wareham L.M.

ETERNAL God, whose changeless will
Encircles all our changing years,
We praise thy love which giveth still
The fruit of joy from seed of tears.

Our founders sought thee: thou wast there
On lonely moor, in prison cell;
Thy presence gave them strength to bear
Reproach, and, suffering, serve thee well.

No more on us is laid the cross
Of sorrow, danger, pain or shame;
They nobly triumphed over loss;
Make us as faithful to thy name.

Grant us thy grace through faith to win
A larger hope, a deeper love;
Steadfast to fight the hosts of sin,
Nor from the Master's footsteps move:

Till faith be sight, our witness done,
Each doubt at rest, hushed every strife,
And all thy Church on earth be one
In growing fulness of thy life.

*J. E. Carpenter**

388

Abridge C.M.

WE love the venerable house
Our founders built to thee:
In heaven are kept their grateful vows
And prayers eternally.

Here holy thoughts a light have shed
From many a radiant face,
And prayers of tender hope have spread
A perfume through the place.

And anxious hearts have pondered here
The mystery of life,
And prayed the eternal Light to clear
Their doubts, and aid their strife.

From humble tenements around
Our forebears came, and then
Within the church a blessing found,
That filled their homes again;

For faith, and peace, and mighty love,
That from the Godhead flow,
Showed them the life of heaven above
Springs from the life below.

They live with God, their homes are dust,
Yet here their children pray,
And in this fleeting lifetime trust
To find the narrow way.

(The following verse may be added, as in the original, on the occasion of an induction)

On him/her who by the altar stands,
On him/her thy blessings send;
Speak through his/her lips thy pure command,
Our Father and our Friend.

*R. W. Emerson**

389

Mainzer L.M.

O THOU, to whom our forebears built
Their altars in the ancient days,
Upon our worship we invoke
The benediction of their praise;

As then their reverent hearts received
The Spirit's gift of flame from thee,
So on our altars kindle now
Fires of ancestral piety.

Thou living, radiant, inward Light!
Whom we today, though dimly, see,
Our guide amid the world we know,
Our hope for what is yet to be,

Break now, in greater majesty,
Upon the minds and hearts that crave
With widening knowledge of the Truth
Triumphant power to seek and save.

God of the ages yet unborn!
Whose clearer presence then shall shine,
When humankind shall live in peace,
And all our life become divine;

O touch our lips that we may be
The messengers of thy swift word,
And with prophetic power proclaim
The growing purpose of the Lord!

*F. M. Eliot**

390

St. George S.M.

COME to thy house, great King!
To thee thy people kneel;
Accept the homage which they bring,
And all thy grace reveal.

Through many a year this place
Service and song hath known,
From hearts that sought thy gracious face
In worship all their own.

The ancient and the new,
The ordered and the free,
The lasting faith, the forward view,
Blend in our rites to thee.

For this our heritage
We own thy fostering hand,
That safely led from age to age
The steadfast, lonely band.

Lord, now their children bless,
Our waiting hearts inspire;
If still we tread the wilderness
Vouchsafe the cloud and fire!

Through triumph and through ill
May we thy presence see;
Make thou our service nobler still,
Our worship worthier thee.

*Anon.**

391

Loughborough 76.76.D.

OUR Father, by whose servants
  Our house was built of old,
Whose hand hath crowned her children
  With blessing manifold,
For thine unfailing mercies
  Far-strewn along our way,
With all who passed before us,
  We praise thy name to-day.

The changeful years unresting
  Their silent course have sped,
New friends forever bringing
  In others' steps to tread;
And some are long forgotten,
  Long spent their hopes and fears;
Safe rest they in thy keeping,
  Who changest not with years.

They reap not where they laboured,
  We reap what they have sown;
Our harvest may be garnered
  By ages yet unknown.
The days of old have dowered us
  With gifts beyond all praise:
Our Father, makes us faithful
  To serve the coming days.

Before us and beside us,
  Still holden in thine hand,
A cloud unseen of witness,
  Our elder friends there stand:
One family unbroken,
  We join, with one acclaim,
One heart, one voice uplifting,
  To glorify thy Name.

*G. W. Briggs**

392

St Matthew C.M.D.

WITHIN this temple, reared of old
By faithful folk and true,
We keep the faith our founders kept,
Their vows to God renew.
They fought the fight, they sank from sight
Beneath the sacred soil;
Though dead, they yet speak on – they live:
In thee they rest from toil!

They nobly battled for the right,
Come many or come few;
The glorious banner of God's truth
Above them proudly flew.
Undauntedly they testified,
Again, and yet again;
They slumbered not on ward or watch:
They fought so bravely then!

Within these hallowed walls were found
Pure witnesses of truth,
Of wise and steadfast womanhood,
And bright and buoyant youth;
Like angels fair, in memory's realm,
They float in holy light,
And softly waft their message down:
"Be steadfast in the right!"

Eternal One! before whose face
We rise – and pass away –
Whose holy will our founders sought,
As we would seek to-day:
Be with us thou, who wert with them;
Lead on by staff or rod;
We ask thy blessing, Lord, this day:
We trust our founders' God.

*A. N. Blatchford**

393

St. Leonard C.M.

O LIGHT, from age to age the same,
For ever living Word,
Here have we felt thy kindling flame,
Thy voice within have heard.

Here holy thought and hymn and prayer
Have winged the spirit's powers,
And made these walls divinely fair –
Thy temple, Lord, and ours.

What visions rise above the years,
What tender memories throng,
Till the eye fills with happy tears,
The heart with grateful song!

Vanish the mists of time and sense;
They come, the loved of old,
And one encircling Providence
Keeps all within thy fold.

Oh, not in vain their toil who wrought
To build faith's freer shrine,
Nor theirs whose steadfast love and thought
Have watched the fire divine.

Burn, holy fire, and shine more wide!
While systems rise and fall,
Faith, hope, and charity abide –
The heart and soul of all.

*F. L. Hosmer**

394

Titchfield 77.77.D.

GRATEFUL hearts and songs of praise
Let us all in tribute raise,
For the love we learned to know
In the days of long ago;
For the love that day by day
Led us gently on our way –
Love of parent, teacher, friend,
And the Love that hath no end.

Ah, what beauty we have seen –
Flowers, and fruits, and grasses green,
Sun and moon, and starlit skies,
And the light of loving eyes!
Ah, what wonders we have heard
Of the great in deed and word,
Souls that, clad with grace divine,
Bright as stars for ever shine!

All from thee, Lord, all from thee –
Glorious things to hear and see,
Treasured memories of the past,
Dearest hopes while life shall last.
So to thee our hearts we give
All our days in love to live;
Keep us, Lord of great and small,
Parent, Teacher, Friend of all.

*W. G. Tarrant**

BAPTISM, CHRISTENING, DEDICATION

395

Childhood 888.6

IT fell upon a summer day,
When Jesus walked in Galilee,
The mothers of the village brought
Their children to his knee.

He took them in his arms, and laid
His hands on each remembered head;
"Suffer these little ones to come
To me," he gently said;

"Forbid them not; unless ye bear
The childlike heart your hearts within,
Unto my kingdom ye may come,
But may not enter in."

Master, I long to enter there;
O let me follow thee, and share
Thy meek and lowly heart, and be
Freed from all worldly care!

All happy thoughts and gentle ways,
And loving kindness daily given,
And freedom through obedience gained,
Make in my heart thy heaven.

O, happy thus to live and move
And love this world where I shall see
God's beauty, goodness and his truth
In all humanity!

*S. A. Brooke**

396

St. Alphege 76.76.

WHAT ask we for the children,
O'er whom life's morning breaks,
Whose eyes in wonder open,
Whose heart to love awakes?

For lives so rich in promise
We ask from God Most High
That loyal, patient service
Their days may beautify

We pray for heavenly wisdom,
High thought and selfless deed,
The kindly, gentle spirit
That comforts those in need.

With strength in life's stern conflict
To front the power of ill,
A glimpse of God's great kingdom,
Their hearts with hope instill.

A restful age of honour,
With loving hands to cheer;
A childlike trust to banish
The sombre shade of fear.

Thus pray we for the children
In life's bright morning glow,
That peaceful, pure, abundant
Their fount of joy may flow.

*A. Chalmers**

397

Church Triumphant/Alstone L.M.

Go forth to life, O child of earth,
Still mindful of thy heavenly birth;
Thou art not here for ease, or sin,
But heaven's noble crown to win.

Though passion's fires are in thy soul,
Thy spirit can their flames control;
Though tempters strong beset thy way,
Thy spirit is more strong than they.

Go on from innocence of youth
To adult pureness, adult truth;
God's angels still are near to save,
And God himself doth help the brave.

Then forth to life, O child of earth,
Be worthy of thy heavenly birth;
For loving service thou art here:
Thy neighbours help, thy God revere.

*S. Longfellow**

398

Aurelia 76.76.D.

To thee, Almighty Father,
This little one we bring,
For love of him who ever
Has been the children's King;
They took him to the Temple
To dedicate to thee
When he was young and helpless:
So, with this babe, do we.

Thy blessing rested on him
Through all his wondrous days;
In lowly, loving service
He ever sought thy praise;
And always little children
Found welcome at his knee;
Their parents brought them gladly:
So, with this babe, do we.

Grant us thy grace, O Father,
  To know this life is lent
To us that we may train it
  To serve thy high intent.
O bless this child and keep him/her
  For ever near to thee;
Thy children ever praise thee:
  So, in this babe, may we.

Ruth Herford

399

Belmont C.M.

BY cool Siloam's shady rill
  How sweet the lily grows!
How sweet the breath beneath the hill
  Of Sharon's dewy rose!

Lo, such the child whose early feet
  The paths of peace have trod;
Whose secret heart, with influence sweet,
  Is upward drawn to God.

O thou, whose infant feet were led
  Within thy Father's shrine,
Whose years, with holiest spirit fed,
  Were all alike divine;

We seek that Spirit's bounteous breath,
  We ask his grace alone,
Through every stage of life till death,
  To keep us still thine own!

*R. Heber**

400

Contemplation/Belmont C.M.

OUR Father, whose creative love
  The gift of life bestows,
Each child of earthly union born
  Thy heavenly likeness shows.

Grant those entrusted with the care
  Of precious life from thee,
Thy grace, that worthy of the gift
  And faithful they may be.

Teach them to meet the growing needs
  Of infant, child, and youth;
To build the body, train the mind
  To know and love the truth;

And, highest task, to feed the soul
  With Christ, the living bread;
That each unfolding life may grow
  Strong in thy paths to tread.

These parents need thy wisdom's light,
  Thy love within their heart;
Bless thou their home, and for their task
  Thy Spirit's grace impart.

Albert F. Bayly

MARRIAGE

401 *Aurelia 76.76.D.*

O LOVE divine and golden,
  Mysterious depth and height,
To thee the world beholden
  Looks up for life and light;
O Love divine and gentle,
  The blesser and the blest,
Beneath whose care parental
  The world lies down in rest.

The fields of earth adore thee,
  The forests sing thy praise,
All living things before thee
  Their holiest anthems raise.
Thou art the joy of gladness;
  The Life of life thou art;
The dew of gentle sadness
  That droppeth on the heart.

O Love divine and tender,
  That through our homes doth move,
Veiled in the softened splendour
  Of holy household love,
Great power without thy blessing
  Were labour without rest,
And poorest homes possessing
  Thy blessedness are blest.

God bless these hands united,
  God bless these heart made one:
Unsevered and unblighted
  May they through life go on;
Here, in earth's home, preparing
  For the bright home above;
And there, for ever sharing
  Its joy, where "God is love."

*J. S. B. Monsell**

(On occasions other than weddings, the final verse might be omitted.)

402

O Perfect Love 11 10.11 10.

O PERFECT Love, all human thought transcending,
  Lowly we kneel in prayer before thy throne,
That theirs may be the love which knows no ending,
  Whom thou for evermore dost join in one.

O perfect Life, be thou their full assurance
  Of tender charity, and steadfast faith,
Of patient hope and quiet, brave endurance,
  With child-like trust that fears not pain nor death.

Grant them the joy which brightens earthly sorrow,
  Grant them the peace which calms all earthly strife,
And to life's day the glorious unknown morrow,
  That dawns upon eternal love and life.

Dorothy F. Gurney

THE LORD'S SUPPER, HOLY COMMUNION

403

St. Agnes/Woodlands 10 10.10 10.

THIS is the hour of banquet and of song;
This is the heav'nly table spread for me;
Here let me feast, and feasting, still prolong
The brief, bright hour of fellowship with thee.

Too soon we rise; we go our several ways;
The feast, though not the love, is past and gone,
The bread and wine consumed: yet all our days
Thou still art here with us our shield and sun.

Feast after feast thus comes and passes by,
Yet, passing, points to the glad feast above,
Giving us foretaste of the festal joy,
The Lord's eternal feast of bliss and love.

H. Bonar

404

Let Us Break Bread *Irregular*

LET us break bread together with the Lord;
Let us break bread together with the Lord:
When I fall on my knees,
With my face to the rising sun,
O Lord, have mercy on me.

Let us drink wine together with the Lord;
Let us drink wine together with the Lord:

Let us praise God together in the Lord;
Let us praise God together in the Lord:

(based on a Negro Spiritual)

405

St. Mary C.M.

O HERE, if ever, God of love,
Let strife and hatred cease,
And every heart harmonious move,
And every thought be peace.

Not here, where met to think of him
  Whose latest thoughts were ours,
Shall mortal passions come to dim
  The prayer devotion pours.

No, gracious Master, not in vain
  Thy life of love hath been;
The peace thou gav'st may yet remain
  Though thou no more art seen.

"Thy kingdom come!" We watch, we wait,
  To hear thy stirring call;
When heaven throws wide the glorious gate,
  And God be all in all.

*Emily Taylor**

406

Dolgelly 66.66.88.

AUTHOR of life divine,
  Who hast a table spread,
Furnished with mystic wine
  And everlasting bread,
Preserve the life thyself hast given,
And feed and train us up for heaven.

Our needy souls sustain
  With fresh supplies of love,
Till all thy life we gain,
  And all thy fulness prove,
And, strengthened by thy perfect grace,
Behold without a veil thy face.

John and Charles Wesley

407

St. Botolph/Martyrdom C.M.

O THOU who this mysterious bread
  Didst in Emmaus break,
Return, herewith our souls to feed,
  And to thy followers speak.

Unseal the volume of thy grace,
  Apply the gospel word,
Open our eyes to see thy face,
  Our hearts to know the Lord.

Of thee communing still, we mourn
  Till thou the veil remove;
Talk with us, and our hearts shall burn
  With flames of fervent love.

Enkindle now the heavenly zeal,
  And make thy mercy known,
And give our pardoned souls to feel
  That God and love are one.

*Charles Wesley**

408

St. Columba 87.87.(iambic)

PUT peace into each other's hands
And like a treasure hold it;
Protect it like a candle flame
With tenderness enfold it.

Put peace into each other's hands
With loving expectation;
Be gentle in your words and ways
In touch with God's creation.

Put peace into each other's hands
Like bread we break for sharing;
Look people warmly in the eye:
Our life is meant for caring.

As at communion, shape your hands
Into a waiting cradle;
The gift of Christ receive, revere,
United round the table.

Put Christ into each other's hands:
He is love's deepest measure;
In love make peace, give peace a chance
And share it like a treasure.

Fred Kaan

409

Ash Grove 12 11.12 11.D.

SENT forth by God's blessing, our true faith confessing,
The People of God from his dwelling take leave.
The supper is ended: O now be extended
The fruits of his service in all who believe.
The seed of his teaching, our hungry souls reaching,
Shall blossom in action for God and for man.
His grace shall incite us, his love shall unite us
To work for his kingdom and further his plan.

With praise and thanksgiving to God everliving,
The task of our everyday life we will face,
Our faith ever sharing, in love ever caring,
Embracing as brothers all men of each race.
One feast that has fed us, one light that has led us,
Unite us as one in his life that we share.
Then may all the living, with praise and thanksgiving,
Give honour to Christ and his name that we bear.

Omer Westendorf

NATIONAL AND INTERNATIONAL

410

Ewing 76.76.D.

O BEAUTIFUL, our country!
Be thine a nobler care
Than all thy wealth of commerce,
Thy harvests waving fair:
Be it thy pride to foster
True justice for the poor;
Be thou to those in bondage
Fair Freedom's open door.

For thee our forebears suffered,
For thee they toiled and prayed;
Upon thy holy altar
Their willing lives they laid.
Thou hast no common birthright,
Grand memories on thee shine:
The blood of noble races
Commingled flows in thine.

O beautiful, our country!
Round thee in love we draw;
Thine be the grace of Freedom,
The majesty of Law.
Be Righteousness thy sceptre,
Justice thy diadem;
And on thy shining forehead
Be Peace the crowning gem!

*F. L. Hosmer**

411

Aberdeen C.M.

LORD, while for humankind we pray,
Of every clime and coast,
O hear us for our native land –
The land we love the most.

O guard our shores from every foe,
With peace our borders bless;
With prosperous times our cities crown,
Our fields with plenteousness.

Unite us in the sacred love
Of knowledge, truth, and thee;
And let our hills and valleys shout
The songs of liberty.

Lord of the nations, thus to thee
Our country we commend;
Be thou her refuge and her trust,
Her everlasting Friend!

*J. R. Wreford**

412

Moscow 664.6664.

GOD bless our native land:
May heaven's protecting hand
Still guard our shore;
May peace her power extend,
Foe be transformed to friend,
And Britain's rights depend
On war no more!

May just and righteous laws
Uphold the public cause,
And bless our isle;
Home of the brave and free,
Thou land of liberty,
We pray that still on thee
Kind heaven may smile.

Nor on this land alone;
But be God's mercies known
From shore to shore;
Lord, make the nations see
That all should kindred be,
And form one family
The wide world o'er!

W. E. Hickson

413

Rhuddlan 87.87.87.

JUDGE eternal, throned in splendour,
Lord of lords and King of kings,
With thy living fire of judgment
Purge this realm of bitter things;
Solace all its wide dominion
With the healing of thy wings.

Still the weary folk are pining
For the hour that brings release;
And the city's crowded clangour
Cries aloud for sin to cease;
And the homesteads and the woodlands
Plead in silence for their peace.

Crown, O God, thine own endeavour;
Cleave our darkness with thy sword;
Feed the faint and hungry nations
With the richness of thy word;
Cleanse the body of our country
Through the glory of the Lord.

*H. S. Holland**

414

King's Lynn 76.76.D.

O GOD of earth and altar,
Bow down and hear our cry;
Our earthly rulers falter,
Our people drift and die;
The walls of gold entomb us,
The swords of scorn divide;
Take not thy thunder from us,
But take away our pride.

From all that terror teaches,
From lies of tongue and pen,
From all the easy speeches
That comfort cruel men,
From sale and profanation
Of honour and the sword,
From sleep and from damnation,
Deliver us, good Lord!

Tie in a living tether
The prince and priest and thrall;
Bind all our lives together;
Smite us and save us all;
In ire and exultation,
Aflame with faith, and free,
Lift up a living nation,
A single sword to thee

G. K. Chesterton

415

Old 124th 10 10.10 10.10.

TURN back, O man, forswear thy foolish ways;
Old now is Earth, and none may count her days;
Yet thou, her child, whose head is crowned with flame,
Still wilt not hear thine inner God proclaim –
"Turn back, O man, forswear thy foolish ways."

Earth might be fair and all men glad and wise.
Age after age their tragic empires rise,
Built while they dream, and in that dreaming weep;
Would Man but wake from out his haunted sleep,
Earth might be fair and all men glad and wise.

Earth shall be fair, and all her people one;
Nor till that hour shall God's whole will be done.
Now, even now, once more from earth to sky
Peals forth in joy Man's old undaunted cry –
"Earth shall be fair, and all her folk be one!"

Clifford Bax

416

Jerusalem LMD Irregular

AND did those feet in ancient time
Walk upon England's mountains green?
And was the holy Lamb of God
On England's pleasant pastures seen?
And did the countenance divine
Shine forth upon our clouded hills?
And was Jerusalem builded here
Among these dark Satanic mills?

Bring me my bow of burning gold!
Bring me my arrows of desire!
Bring me my spear! O clouds, unfold!
Bring me my chariot of fire!
I will not cease from mental fight,
Nor shall my sword sleep in my hand,
Till we have built Jerusalem
In England's green and pleasant land.

William Blake

417

Alford 76.86 D.

THE founders built this city
  In ages long ago,
And busy in its crowded streets
  They hurried to and fro;
The children played around them
  And sang the songs of old
Till, one by one, they fell asleep,
  All gathered in thy fold.

Yet still the city standeth
  A busy place as then,
And parents' love makes happy home
  For children yet again;
O God of Ages, help us
  Such citizens to be
That children's children here may sing
  The songs of liberty.

Let all the people praise thee,
  Give all thy saving health,
Or vain the worker's strong right arm
  And vain the banker's wealth;
Send forth thy light to banish
  The shadows and the shame,
Till all the civic virtues shine
  Around our city's name.

A commonweal of people
  United, great and small,
Upon our banner blazoned be
  The charter, "Each for all!"
Nor let us cease from struggle
  Nor weary sheathe the sword,
Until this city is become
  The city of the Lord.

*W. G. Tarrant**

418

Galilee/Merthyr Tydvil *L.M. or L.M.D.*

THESE things shall be! a nobler race
Than e'er the world hath known shall rise,
With flame of freedom in their souls
And light of knowledge in their eyes.

They shall be gentle, brave, and strong
To spill no drop of blood, but dare
All that may make them stewards true
Of earth and fire and sea and air.

They shall be simple in their homes
And splendid in their public ways,
Filling the mansions of the state
With music and with hymns of praise.

Nation with nation, land with land,
Unarmed shall live as neighbours free;
In every heart and brain shall throb
The pulse of one humanity.

New arts shall bloom with power to move,
And mightier music thrill the skies,
And every life shall be a song,
When all the earth is paradise.

There shall be no more sin nor shame,
Though pain and passion may not die;
For we shall be at one with God
In bonds of firm necessity.

*J. A. Symonds**

419

Aberystwyth *77.77 D.*

THOUGH it is our boast that we
Come of parents brave and free,
If there breathe on earth a slave,
Are we truly free and brave?
If we do not feel the chain
When it works another's pain
Are we not base slaves indeed,
Slaves unworthy to be freed?

Is true freedom but to break
Fetters for own dear sake,
And with leathern hearts forget
That we owe the world a debt?
No, true freedom is to share
All the chains that others wear,
And with heart and hand to be
Earnest to make others free.

They are slaves who fear to speak
For the fallen and the weak;
They are slaves who will not choose
Hatred, scoffing, and abuse,
Rather than in silence shrink
From the truth they needs must think;
They are slaves who dare not be
In the right with two or three.

*J. R. Lowell**

420

St. Cecilia 66.66.

THY Kingdom come, O Lord,
  Wide circling as the sun;
Fulfil of old thy word
  And make the nations one;

One in the bond of peace,
  The service glad and free
Of truth and righteousness,
  Of love and equity.

Speed, speed the longed-for time
  Foretold by raptured seers –
The prophecy sublime,
  The hope of all the years;

Till rise at last, its wall
  And firm foundations broad,
The commonwealth of all,
  The city of our God.

*F. L. Hosmer**

421

St. Asaph C.M.D.

ETERNAL God, whose power upholds
Both flower and flaming star,
To whom there is no here nor there,
No time, no near nor far,
No alien race, no foreign shore,
No child unsought, unknown,
O send us forth, thy prophets true,
To make all lands thine own!

O God of truth, whom science seeks
And reverent souls adore,
Who lightest every earnest mind
Of every clime and shore,
Dispel the gloom of error's night,
Of ignorance and fear,
Until true wisdom from above
Shall make life's pathway clear!

O God of love, whose spirit wakes
In every human breast,
Whom love, and love alone, can know,
In whom all hearts find rest,
Help us to spread thy gracious reign,
Till greed and hate shall cease,
And kindness dwell in human hearts,
And all the earth find peace!

Henry Hallam Tweedy

422

Schmücke dich 88.88.D.

ONE world this, for all its sorrow;
One world shaping one tomorrow;
One humanity, though riven –
To us all a world is given.
From one world there is no turning;
For one world the prophet's yearning.
One, the world of poets, sages;
One world, goal of all the ages.

One, our world from the beginning;
One, the world we would be winning;
World so eagerly expected;
World so recklessly rejected.
One, enfolding every nation;
One, our mightiest creation:
Dream, to guide the mind's endeavour;
Hope, to hold the heart for ever.

One world, land and air and ocean;
One, upheld by our devotion.
One, as common folk have willed it;
One, as government can build it.
World of friendly ways and faces,
Cherished arts and honoured races.
One world, free in word and science;
All folk free, its firm reliance.

*Vincent B. Silliman**

423

St. Stephen C.M.

O GOD! the darkness roll away
Which clouds the human soul,
And let thy bright and holy day
Speed onward to its goal!

Let every hateful passion die
Which makes of kindred foes,
And war no longer raise its cry
To mar the world's repose.

How long shall glory still be found
  In scenes of cruel strife,
Where misery walks, a giant crowned,
  Crushing the flowers of life?

O hush, great God, the sounds of war,
  And make thy children feel
That we with thee are nobler far
  Who toil for human weal.

Let faith, and hope, and charity
  Go forth through all the earth;
And we in holy friendship be
  True to our heavenly birth.

*W. Gaskell**

424

Vision Irregular

IT is God who holds the nations in the hollow of his hand;
It is God whose light is shining in the darkness of the land;
It is God who builds his City on the Rock and not on sand:
  May the living God be praised!

It is God whose purpose summons us to use the present hour;
Who recalls us to our senses when a nation's life turns sour;
In the discipline of freedom we shall know his saving power:
  May the living God be praised!

When a thankful nation, looking back, has cause to celebrate
Those who win our admiration by their service to the state;
When self-giving is a measure of the greatness of the great:
  May the living God be praised!

He reminds us every sunrise that the world is ours on lease:
For the sake of life tomorrow may our love for it increase;
May all races live together, share its riches, be at peace:
  May the living God be praised!

F. Pratt Green

425

Luther King House *86.88.6.*

"I HAVE a dream," a man once said,
"Where all is perfect peace:
Where men and women, black and white,
Stand hand in hand, and all unite
In freedom and in love".

But in this world of bitter strife
The dream can often fade:
Reality seems dark as night,
We catch but glimpses of the light
Christ sheds on humankind.

Fierce persecution, war and hate
Are raging everywhere:
Through struggle and through sacrifice
God's people pay the costly price
Of standing for the right.

So dream your dreams and sing your songs,
But never be content;
For thoughts and words don't ease the pain,
Unless there's action, all is vain,
Faith proves itself in deeds.

Lord, grant us vision, make us strong,
And help us do your will;
Nor let us rest until we see
Your love throughout humanity
Uniting us in peace.

Pamela J. Pettitt

426

Finlandia 11 10.11 10.11 10.

THIS is my song, O God of all the nations,
 A song of peace for lands afar and mine;
This is my home, the country where my heart is,
 Here are my hopes, my dreams, my holy shrine;
But other hearts in other lands are beating
 With hopes and dreams as true and high as mine.

My country's skies are bluer than the ocean,
 And sunlight beams on clover leaf and pine;
But other lands have sunlight, too, and clover,
 And skies are everywhere as blue as mine.
O hear my song, thou God of all the nations,
 A song of peace for their land and for mine.

Lloyd Stone

TIMES AND SEASONS

MORNING

427

Morning Hymn L.M.

AWAKE, my soul, and with the sun
Thy daily stage of duty run;
Shake off dull sloth, and joyful rise
To pay thy morning sacrifice.

All praise to thee who safe hast kept,
And hast refreshed me while I slept;
Grant, Lord, when I from death shall wake,
I may of endless light partake.

Lord, I my vows to thee renew;
Scatter my sins as morning dew;
Guard my first springs of thought and will,
And with thyself my spirit fill.

Direct, control, suggest this day
All I design, or do, or say,
That all my powers, with all their might,
In thy sole glory may unite.

Praise God, from whom all blessings flow;
Praise him, all creatures here below;
Praise him, ye heavenly hosts above;
Praise him, my soul, for all his love!

*T. Ken**

428

Melcombe L.M.

NEW every morning is the love
Our wakening and uprising prove;
Through sleep and darkness safely brought,
Restored to life, and power, and thought.

New mercies, each returning day,
Hover around us while we pray;
New perils past, new sins forgiven,
New thoughts of God, new hopes of heaven.

If on our daily course our mind
Be set to hallow all we find,
New treasures still, of countless price,
God will provide for sacrifice.

Old friends, old scenes will lovelier be,
As more of heaven in each we see;
Some softening gleam of love and prayer
Shall dawn on every cross and care.

The trivial round, the common task,
Will furnish all we ought to ask;
Room to deny ourselves, a road
To bring us daily nearer God.

Only, O Lord, in thy dear love
Fit us for perfect rest above;
And help us, this and every day,
To live more nearly as we pray.

J. Keble

429

Selborne/Winchester New L.M.

NOW with creation's morning song
Let us, as children of the day,
With wakened heart and purpose strong,
The works of darkness cast away.

Oh, may the morn so pure, so clear,
Its holy calm in us instil,
A guileless mind, a heart sincere,
Simplicity of word and will.

And ever, as the day glides by,
May we the busy senses rein,
Keep guard upon the hand and eye,
Nor let the conscience suffer stain.

Grant us, O God, in love to thee,
Clear eyes to measure things below,
Faith, the invisible to see,
And wisdom, thee in all to know.

Breviary, trans. E. Caswall, altered S. Longfellow

430

Wolvercote 76.76.D

THE morning hangs a signal
Upon the mountain crest,
While all the sleeping valleys
In silent darkness rest.
From peak to peak it flashes,
It laughs along the sky,
Till glory of the sunlight
On all the land doth lie.

Above the generations
The lonely prophets rise,
While truth flings dawn and day-star
Within their glowing eyes;
And other eyes, beholding,
Are kindled from that light,
And dawn becometh morning;
The darkness put to flight.

The soul hath lifted moments,
  Above the drift of days,
When life's great meaning breaketh
  In sunrise on our ways.
Behold the radiant token
  Of faith above all fear;
Night shall be lost in splendour
  And morning shall appear!

W. C. Gannett

431

Epworth/Glasgow C.M.

O LORD of life, thy quickening voice
  Awakes my morning song;
In grateful words I would rejoice
  That I to thee belong.

I see thy light, I feel thy wind;
  Earth is thy uttered word:
Whatever wakes my heart and mind,
  Thy presence is, my Lord.

Therefore I choose my highest part,
  And turn my face to thee;
Therefore I stir my inmost heart
  To worship fervently.

Lord, let me live and act this day,
  Still rising from the dead;
Lord, make my spirit quick to pray:
  Give me my daily bread.

Within my heart, speak, Lord, speak on,
  My heart alive to keep
Till the night comes, and, labour done,
  In thee I fall asleep.

*G. Macdonald**

432

Warrington LM

GOD of the morning, at whose voice
The cheerful sun makes haste to rise,
And like a giant doth rejoice
To run his journey through the skies!

From the fair chambers of the east
The circuit of his race begins;
And without weariness or rest,
Round the whole earth he flies and shines.

Oh, like the sun may I fulfil
The appointed duties of the day;
With ready mind and active will
March on, and keep my heavenly way.

Lord thy commands are clean and pure,
Enlightening our beclouded eyes;
Thy judgements just, thy promise sure;
Thy gospel makes the simple wise.

Give me thy counsels for my guide,
And then receive me to thy bliss:
All my desires and hope beside
Are faint and cold compared with this.

*Isaac Watts**

433

Bunessan 55.54.D.

MORNING has broken
Like the first morning,
Blackbird has spoken
Like the first bird.
Praise for the singing!
Praise for the morning!
Praise for them, springing
Fresh from the word!

Sweet the rain's new fall
Sunlit from heaven,
Like the first dewfall
  On the first grass.
    Praise for the sweetness
    Of the wet garden,
    Sprung in completeness
  Where his feet pass.

Mine is the sunlight!
Mine is the morning
Born of the one light
  Eden saw play!
    Praise with elation,
    Praise every morning,
    God's re-creation
  Of the new day!

Eleanor Farjeon

434

Bunessan 55.54.D.

As the sun rises,
I stand in darkness:
Where light is shining,
I am in gloom.
Who shuts its rays out,
Who dims my vision,
Who keeps me prisoner
In this locked room?

I am my keeper,
I am my jailer,
I am the judge who
Locks me in chains.
Fearing my freedom
To live like Jesus,
I have lost all life –
Nothing remains.

Now I will break free
From my heart's bondage,
Follow the vision
Jesus enshrined,
Give up my false pride,
Offer my true self,
Welcome the Spirit
No-one can bind.

Now the sun rises,
Driving the darkness
Out of my thinking –
Let it depart.
Now I am singing,
Freedom is winging
All through our worship,
From heart to heart.

Peter Galbraith

EVENING

435

Angelus L.M.

AGAIN, as evening's shadow falls,
We gather in these hallowed walls;
And vesper hymn and vesper prayer
Rise mingling on the holy air.

May struggling hearts that seek release
Here find the rest of God's own peace;
And, strengthened here by hymn and prayer,
Lay down the burden and the care.

O God, our light, to thee we bow;
Within all shadows standest thou;
Give deeper calm than night can bring;
Give lovelier songs than lips can sing.

Life's tumult we must meet again;
We cannot at the shrine remain;
But in the spirit's secret cell
May hymn and prayer for ever dwell.

*S. Longfellow**

436

St. Anatolius 76.76.88.

THE day is past and over,
All thanks, O Lord, to thee;
We pray thee now that sinless
The hours of dark may be.
O Father, keep us in thy sight,
And guard us through the coming night.

The joys of day are over;
We lift our hearts to thee,
And ask thee that offenceless
The hours of dark may be.
O Father, keep us in thy sight,
And guard us through the coming night.

The toils of day are over;
We raise the hymn to thee,
And ask that free from peril
The hours of dark may be.
O Father, keep us in thy sight,
And guard us through the coming night.

Be thou our soul's preserver,
For thou alone dost know
How many are the perils
Through which we have to go.
O loving Father, hear our call,
And guard and save us from them all.

*Anatolius, trans. J. M. Neale**

437

St. Clement 98.98.

THE day thou gavest, Lord, is ended,
The darkness falls at thy behest;
To thee our morning hymns ascended,
Thy praise shall sanctify our rest.

We thank thee that thy Church unsleeping,
While earth rolls onward into light,
Through all the world her watch is keeping,
And rests not now by day or night.

As o'er each continent and island
The dawn leads on another day,
The voice of prayer is never silent,
Nor dies the strain of praise away.

The sun, that bids us rest, is waking
Our kindred 'neath the western sky,
And hour by hour fresh lips are making
Thy wondrous doings heard on high.

So be it, Lord; thy throne shall never,
Like earth's proud empires, pass away;
Thy kingdom stands and grows for ever,
Till all thy creatures own thy sway.

*J. Ellerton**

438

Ar hyd y nos *84.84.8884.*

GOD that madest earth and heaven,
Darkness and light;
Who the day for toil hast given,
For rest the night;
May thine angel-guard defend us,
Slumber sweet thy mercy send us,
Holy dreams and hopes attend us
This livelong night.

When we in the morn awaken,
Guide us thy way;
Keep our love and truth unshaken
In work and play;
In our daily task be near us,
In temptation keep and hear us,
And with holy counsel cheer us
The livelong day.

Guard us waking, guard us sleeping,
  And, when we die,
May we in thy mighty keeping
  All peaceful lie;
Thou wilt not in death forsake us,
But to fuller life wilt wake us,
And to nobler service take us
  With thee on high.

R. Heber and others

439

Abends/Hursley L.M.

SUN of my soul, thou Saviour dear,
It is not night if thou be here;
Oh, may no earth-born cloud arise
To hide thee from thy servant's eyes!

Abide with me from morn till eve,
For without thee I cannot live;
Abide with me when night is nigh,
For without thee I dare not die.

If some poor wandering child of thine
Have spurned to-day the voice divine,
Now, Lord, the gracious work begin;
Let him no more lie down in sin.

Watch by the sick; enrich the poor
With blessings from thy boundless store;
Be every mourner's sleep to-night,
Like infants' slumbers, pure and light.

Come near and bless us when we wake,
Ere through the world our way we take;
Till in the ocean of thy love
We lose ourselves in heaven above.

J. Keble

440

Innsbruck 776.778.

THE duteous day now closeth,
Each flower and tree reposeth,
Shade creeps o'er wild and wood;
Let us, as night is falling,
On God our Maker calling,
Give thanks to him, the Giver good.

Now all the heavenly splendour
Breaks forth in starlight tender
From myriad worlds unknown;
And we, the marvel seeing,
Forget our selfish being,
For joy of beauty not our own.

Our care we drown it yonder,
Lost in the abyss of wonder;
To heaven our souls then steal;
This life one disesteemeth,
The day it is that dreameth,
That doth from truth our vision seal.

Awhile our mortal blindness
May miss God's loving-kindness,
And grope in faithless strife;
But when life's day is over
Shall death's fair night discover
The fields of everlasting life

*R. Bridges**

441

Tallis' Canon L.M.

GLORY to thee, my God, this night,
For all the blessings of the light!
Keep me, O keep me, King of kings,
Beneath thine own almighty wings!

The moments that to waste have run,
The ills that I this day have done,
Forgive, that with the world and thee
I, ere I sleep, at peace may be.

O may my soul on thee repose,
And may sweet sleep mine eyelids close;
Sleep that shall me more vigorous make
To serve my God when I awake!

Teach me to live, that I may dread
The grave as little as my bed:
Teach me to die, that so I may
With joy behold the endless day.

Praise God, from whom all blessings flow;
Praise him, all creatures here below;
Praise him, ye heavenly hosts above;
Praise him, my soul, for all his love!

*T. Ken**

OLD AND NEW YEAR

442

Patmos 77.77.

BACKWARD looking o'er the past,
Forward, too, with eager gaze,
Stand we here to-day, O God,
At the parting of the ways.

Tenderest thoughts our bosoms fill;
Memories all bright and fair
Seem to float on spirit wings,
Downward through the silent air.

Hark! through all their music rings –
Is that not a voice of cheer?
'Tis the voice of hope which sings,
"Happy be the coming year."

Father, comes that voice from thee,
Swells it with thy meaning vast,
Good in all thy future stored,
Fairer than in all the past!

J. W. Chadwick

443

Deus tuorum militum L.M.

RING out, wild bells, to the wild sky,
The flying cloud, the frosty light;
The year is dying in the night;
Ring out, wild bells, and let him die.

Ring out the old, ring in the new,
Ring, happy bells, across the snow;
The year is going, let him go;
Ring out the false, ring in the true.

Ring out a slowly dying cause,
And ancient forms of party strife;
Ring in the nobler modes of life,
With gentler manners, purer laws.

Ring out false pride in place and blood,
The civic slander and the spite;
Ring in the love of truth and right,
Ring in the common love of good.

Ring out old shapes of foul disease;
Ring out the narrowing lust of gold;
Ring out the thousand wars of old,
Ring in the thousand years of peace.

Ring in the valiant soul and free,
The larger heart, the kindlier hand;
Ring out the darkness of the land,
Ring in the Christ that is to be.

*Alfred Tennyson**

444

Newcastle 86.886.

ANOTHER year of labour gone,
And now, O Lord, we meet
To bless thee for the light that shone
And led us with its radiance on,
And brought us to thy feet.

To thee we raise no mournful song,
  No note of sad despair,
But joyful praise from heart and tongue;
For all our hopes to thee belong,
  All mercies rich and rare.

As in a land of summer flowers,
  Our steps have wander'd free;
And glad and bright have been the hours
When we have felt our noblest powers
  Awake to follow thee.

Thy waters clear have sung in rills
  Beside our dusty way,
And borne the music of the hills
Along the vale of human ills,
  A song of golden day.

O Father, help thy people here,
  As oft in seasons gone,
To hear the voice that conquers fear
And fills the soul with heavenly cheer,
  While months and years roll on.

For thine is all the work we do,
  All light and grace are thine;
From day to day our faith renew
And keep us to the truth more true,
  More full of love divine.

J. Bell

445

Monkland 77.77.

PRAISE to God and thanks we bring!
Hearts bow down, and voices sing
Praises to the glorious One,
All his year of wonder done!

Praise him for his budding green,
April's resurrection-scene;
Praise him for his shining hours,
Starring all the land with flowers!

Praise him for his summer rain,
Feeding, day and night, the grain;
Praise him for his tiny seed,
Holding all his world shall need!

Praise him for his garden root,
Meadow grass and orchard fruit;
Praise for hills and valleys broad –
Each the table of the Lord!

Praise him now for snowy rest,
Falling soft on Nature's breast;
Praise for happy dreams of birth
Brooding in the quiet earth!

For his year of wonder done,
Praise to the all-glorious One!
Hearts bow down, and voices sing
Alleluia to our King!

W. C. Gannett

446

Eisenach L.M.

GREAT God! we sing that mighty hand
By which supported still we stand;
The opening year thy mercy shows;
Thy mercy crowns it till its close.

By day, by night, at home, abroad,
Still are we guarded by our God;
By his incessant bounty fed,
By his unerring counsel led.

With grateful hearts the past we own;
The future, all to us unknown,
We to thy guardian care commit,
And peaceful leave before thy feet.

In scenes exalted or depressed
Thou art our joy, and thou our rest;
Thy goodness all our hopes shall raise,
Adored through all our changing days.

When death shall interrupt these songs,
And seal in silence mortal tongues,
Our helper God, in whom we trust,
In better worlds shall be our boast.

Philip Doddridge

447

University C.M.

WELCOME from God, O glad new year!
  Thy paths all yet untrod,
But prophecy and promise, all –
  O glad new year of God!

Another year of setting suns,
  Of stars by night revealed,
Of springing grass, of tender buds
  By winter's snow concealed.

Another year of summer's glow,
  Of autumn's gold and brown,
Of waving fields, and ripened fruit
  The branches weighing down.

Another year of happy work,
  That better is than play;
Of simple cares, and love that grows
  More deep from day to day

Another year of family joy,
  And childhood's blessèd ways;
Of thinker's thought, and prophet's dreams,
  And poet's tender lays.

Another year at beauty's feast,
  At every moment spread;
Of silent hours when grow distinct
  The voices of the dead.

Another year to follow hard
  Where better souls have trod;
Another year of life's delight;
  Another year of God!

*J. W. Chadwick**

448

Innocents 77.77.

BLESS, O Lord, the opening year
To the souls assembled here;
Clothe thy words with power divine,
Make us willing to be thine.

Where thou hast thy work begun,
Give new strength the race to run;
Scatter darkness, doubts, and fears;
Wipe away the mourner's tears.

Bless us all, both old and young;
Call forth praise from every tongue;
Let our whole assembly prove
All thy power and all thy love.

John Newton

449

Father, let me dedicate 75.75.D.

FATHER, let me dedicate
All this year to thee,
In whatever worldly state
Thou wilt have me be;
Not from sorrow, pain, or care,
Freedom dare I claim;
This alone shall be my prayer –
Glorify thy Name.

Can a child presume to choose
Where or how to live?
Can a Father's love refuse
All the best to give?
More thou givest every day
Than the best can claim,
Nor withholdest aught that may
Glorify thy Name.

If thou callest to the cross,
And its shadows come,
Turning all my gain to loss,
Shrouding heart and home;
Let me think how thy dear Son
To his glory came,
And in deepest woe pray on –
Glorify thy Name.

If in mercy thou wilt spare
Joys that yet are mine;
If on life, serene and fair,
Brighter rays may shine;
Let my glad heart, while it sings,
Thee in all proclaim,
And whate'er the future brings,
Glorify thy Name.

*L. Tuttiett**

THE SEASONS

450

Beulah/St. Matthew C.M.D.

ALL beautiful the march of days,
As seasons come and go;
The hand that shaped the rose hath wrought
The crystal of the snow;
Hath sent the hoary frost of heaven,
The flowing waters sealed,
And laid a silent loveliness
On hill and wood and field.

O'er white expanses sparkling pure
The radiant morns unfold;
The solemn splendours of the night
Burn brighter through the cold;
Life mounts in every throbbing vein,
Love deepens round the hearth,
And clearer sounds the angel hymn,
"Good-will to men on earth."

O thou from whose unfathomed law
  The year in beauty flows,
Thyself the vision passing by
  In crystal and in rose,
Day unto day doth utter speech,
  And night to night proclaim,
In ever-changing words of light,
  The wonder of thy Name.

Frances W. Wile

451

Crüger 76.76 D.

LORD of the silent winter,
  Beneath whose skies of grey
The frost-bound fields lie cheerless,
  But wait a brighter day;
If human hearts are dreary,
  By mists of sorrow chilled,
Give patience to the weary,
  Till they with peace be filled!

Lord of the joyous spring-time,
  When leaves and buds appear,
And lengthening days of beauty
  Renew the softened year;
Breathe on our hearts in blessing,
  Away our sadness roll;
And send, all pain redressing,
  A spring-time to the soul!

Lord of the glowing summer,
  When waves the corn on high,
And fruits in valleys ripen
  Beneath a cloudless sky;
Shine on our hearts' endeavour
  To give our strength to thee,
That in our spirits ever
  A richer life may be!

Lord of the bounteous autumn,
  When vineyards yield their store,
And golden sheaves, new-gathered,
  Pass to the garner door:
Grant now a full fruition
  To every seed of truth,
Which fell, with blessèd mission,
  Upon our souls in youth!

Lord of the changing seasons,
  Lord of our passing days,
Wake thou in us abundance
  Of duty, love, and praise:
That hearts of wintry sadness
  May feel the breath of spring,
And summer's time of gladness
  The autumn glories bring!

D. Agate

452

Morning Light 76.76.D.

COME, sing with holy gladness,
  High Alleluias sing;
Lift up your hearts and voices
  With new-awakened spring.
Sing, all young men and women,
  Today your hymn of praise,
With old folk and with children,
  The song of triumph raise.

The time of resurrection!
  Earth sings it all abroad;
The Passover of gladness,
  The Passover of God!
The sign of life eternal
  Is writ on earth and sky,
The hope for ever vernal,
  Of Life the victory.

Now let the heavens be joyful;
The seas their bright waves swell,
Let the round world keep triumph
With all that therein dwell!
Now let the seen and unseen
In one glad anthem blend,
Let all our hearts be risen
To life that hath no end!

*J. J. Daniell**

453

Ruth 65.65.D.

SUMMER suns are glowing
Over land and sea,
Happy light is flowing
Bountiful and free.
Everything rejoices
In the mellow rays,
All earth's thousand voices
Swell the psalm of praise.

God's free mercy streameth
Over all the world,
And his banner gleameth
Everywhere unfurled.
Broad and deep and glorious
As the heaven above,
Shines in might victorious
His eternal Love.

Lord, upon our blindness
Thy pure radiance pour;
For thy loving-kindness
Make us love thee more.
And when clouds are drifting
Dark across our sky,
Then, the veil uplifting,
Father, be thou nigh.

We will never doubt thee,
Though thou veil thy light:
Life is dark without thee,
Death with thee is bright.
Light of Light, shine o'er us
On our pilgrim way,
Go thou still before us
To the endless day.

W. W. How

HARVEST THANKSGIVING

454

St. George (Windsor) 77.77.D.

COME, ye thankful people, come,
Raise the song of Harvest-home;
All is safely gathered in,
Ere the winter storms begin;
God, our Maker, doth provide
For our wants to be supplied:
Come to God's own temple, come,
Raise the song of Harvest-home!

All the blessings of the field,
All the stores the gardens yield,
All the fruits in full supply,
Ripened 'neath the summer sky;
All that spring with bounteous hand
Scatters o'er the smiling land,
All that liberal autumn pours
From her rich o'erflowing stores;

These to thee, our God, we owe,
Source whence all our blessings flow;
And for these our souls shall raise
Grateful vows and solemn praise.
Come, then, thankful people, come,
Raise the song of Harvest-home;
Come to God's own temple, come,
Raise the song of Harvest-home.

H. Alford, Anna L. Barbauld and others

455

Bounty 9.8.9.8. *(anapaestic)*

NOW sing we a song for the harvest:
  Thanksgiving and honour and praise
For all that the bountiful Giver
  Hath given to gladden our days;

For grasses of upland and lowland,
  For fruits of the garden and field,
For gold which the mine and the furrow
  To delver and husbandman yield.

And thanks for the harvest of beauty,
  For that which the hands cannot hold,
The harvest eyes only can gather
  And only our hearts can enfold:

We reap it on mountain and moorland;
  We glean it from meadow and lea;
We garner it in from the cloudland;
  We bind it in sheaves from the sea.

But now we sing deeper and higher
  Of harvests that eye cannot see;
They ripen on mountains of duty,
  Are reaped by the brave and the free:

And these have been gathered and garnered –
  Some golden with honour and gain,
And some, as with heart's blood, are reddened,
  The harvests of sorrow and pain.

O thou who art Lord of the harvest,
  The Giver who gladdens our days,
Our hearts are for ever repeating
  Thanksgiving and honour and praise.

*J. W. Chadwick and W. C. Gannett**

456

Wir pflügen 76.76.D.66.84.

WE plough the fields, and scatter
  The good seed on the land,
But it is fed and watered
  By God's almighty hand;
He sends the snow in winter,
  The warmth to swell the grain,
The breezes and the sunshine,
  And soft refreshing rain.

All good gifts around us
Are sent from heaven above;
Then thank the Lord, O thank the Lord,
For all his love!

He only is the Maker
  Of all things near and far;
He paints the wayside flower,
  He lights the evening star;
The winds and waves obey him,
  By him the birds are fed;
Much more to us, his children,
  He gives our daily bread.

We thank thee then, O Father,
  For all things bright and good,
The seed-time and the harvest,
  Our life, our health, our food.
Accept the gifts we offer
  For all thy love imparts,
And, what thou most desirest,
  Our humble, thankful hearts.

Matthias Claudius, trans. Jane M. Campbell

457

Malvern/Moscow 664.6664.

THE God of harvest praise;
In loud thanksgiving raise
Hand, heart, and voice:
The valleys laugh and sing,
Forests and mountains ring,
The plains their tribute bring,
The streams rejoice.

Yea, bless his holy Name,
And joyous thanks proclaim
Through all the earth:
To glory in your lot
Is comely; but be not
God's benefits forgot
Amid your mirth.

The God of harvest praise;
Hands, hearts, and voices raise,
With sweet accord:
From field to garner throng,
Bearing your sheaves along,
And in your harvest-song
Bless ye the Lord.

*J. Montgomery**

458

Thanksgiving/Breslau L.M.

WE praise thee, God, for harvests earned,
The fruits of labour garnered in;
But praise thee more for soil unturned
From which the yield is yet to win.

We praise thee for the harbour's lee,
And moorings safe in waters still;
But more for leagues of open sea,
Where favouring gales our canvas fill.

We praise thee for the journey's end,
The welcome rest, the food and cheer;
But more for lengthening roads that wend
Through dust and heat to hill-tops clear.

We praise thee for the conflicts won,
For captured strongholds of the foe;
But more for fields whereon the sun
Lights us when we to battle go.

We praise thee for life's gathered gains,
The blessings that our cup o'erbrim;
But more for pledge of what remains
Past the horizon's utmost rim!

*J. C. Adams**

459

Shipston 87.87

GOD, whose farm is all creation,
Take the gratitude we give;
Take the finest of our harvest,
Crops we grow that all may live.

Take our ploughing, seeding, reaping,
Hopes and fears of sun and rain,
All our thinking, planning, waiting,
Ripened in this fruit and grain.

All our labour, all our watching,
All our calendar of care,
In these crops of your creation,
Take, O God: they are our prayer.

John Arlott

460

Day of Rest 76.76.D.

LORD of the living harvest,
That whitens o'er the plain,
Where angels soon shall gather
Their sheaves of golden grain;
Accept these hands to labour,
These hearts to trust and love,
And deign with them to hasten
Thy kingdom from above.

As labourers in thy vineyard,
Send us out, Lord, to be
Content to bear the burden
Of weary days for thee;
Content to ask no wages,
When thou shalt call us home,
But to have shared the travail
Which makes thy kingdom come.

Breathe on us, Holy Spirit,
Illumine with thy light;
Clothe us in spotless raiment,
In linen clean and white;
Within thy sacred temple
Be with us, where we stand,
And sanctify thy people,
Throughout this happy land.

*J. B. S. Monsell**

461

Angel Voices 85.85.843

FLOWERS and fruit of field and garden
Offered up in praise:
Harvest comes each year to gladden,
Thrill, delight, amaze.
All who ponder Nature's mystery
Sense the mastery
God displays.

Plough and furrow, hoe and border
  Are not God's alone:
We have grafted on to Nature
  Efforts of our own.
Many seeds that have through ages
    Brought great riches
    We have sown.

All that makes our life worth living
  Comes about like this:
Hope is fruitful, toil fulfilling
  When our skilfulness
Joins with God to make together
    Works that ever
    Bring success.

In the laden harvest-table
  Let us therefore find
Of this partnership a symbol –
  God with us combined:
Grace of God and our endeavour,
    Faith and labour
    Intertwined.

Let us also freely offer
  Love and zest and mirth;
Add to Nature's cornucopia
  Fruits of human worth:
God with us together reaping
    Hope-inspiring
    Joy on earth.

Praise to God who makes things ripen,
  Praise to those who sow;
Praise to soil and rain and sunshine,
  Praise to plough and hoe.
People, Nature, God, together
    Let a greater
    Goodness grow.

William Radice

462

Ar Hyd y Nos 84.84.888.4.

WELCOME harvest now beginning
Over the land,
Golden fields of summer riches
Wait for your hand;
Farmers riding mighty combines
Toil by moonlight, toil by sunshine
Bringing home our good earth's bounty
At your command.

Thanks and praise we bring in plenty
This Lammas-tide,
That the miracle of harvest
Food does provide;
But, O God, divine creator,
Show us how to love our neighbour,
That the fruits of earth may feed your
People world-wide.

Clifford Martin Reed

CLOSE OF WORSHIP

463

St. Mabyn 87.87.

PART in peace! is day before us?
Praise his Name for life and light;
Are the shadows lengthening o'er us?
Bless his care who guards the night.

Part in peace! with deep thanksgiving,
Rendering, as we homeward tread,
Gracious service to the living,
Tranquil memory to the dead.

Part in peace! such are the praises
God our Maker loveth best;
Such the worship that upraises
Human hearts to heavenly rest.

Sarah F. Adams

464

Horsley C.M.

THE Lord be with us as we bow
His blessing to receive;
His gift of peace he will bestow,
Before his courts we leave.

The Lord be with us as we walk
Along our homeward road;
In silent thought or friendly talk
Our hearts be near to God.

The Lord be with us till the night
Enfold our day of rest;
Be he of every heart the light,
Of every home the guest.

The Lord be with us through the hours
Of slumber calm and deep,
Protect our homes, renew our powers,
And guard his people's sleep.

*J. Ellerton**

465

Buckland 77.77.

FATHER, now our prayer is said,
Lay thy hand upon our head;
Pleasures pass from day to day,
But we know that love will stay.

While we sleep it will be near;
We shall wake and find it here;
We shall feel it in the air,
When we say our morning prayer.

And when things are sad and wrong,
Then we know that love is strong;
When we ache, or when we weep,
Then we know that love is deep.

Love is old, and love is new;
Love outlasteth firm and true;
May our love for ever be
Perfected, O Lord, in thee.

*W. B. Rands**

466

Ellers 10 10.10 10.

FATHER, again to thy dear Name we raise
With one accord our parting hymn of praise;
We stand to bless thee ere our worship cease,
Then, lowly kneeling, wait thy word of peace.

Grant us thy peace upon our homeward way;
With thee began, with thee shall end the day;
Guard thou the lips from sin, the hearts from shame,
That in this house have called upon thy Name.

Grant us thy peace, Lord, through the coming night,
Turn thou for us its darkness into light;
From harm and danger keep thy children free,
For dark and light are both alike to thee.

Grant us thy peace throughout our earthly life,
Our balm in sorrow, and our stay in strife;
Then, when thy voice shall bid our conflict cease,
Call us, O Lord, to thine eternal peace.

*J. Ellerton**

467

Ellers 10 10.10 10.

O GOD our Father, who dost make us one,
Heart bound to heart in love of thy dear Son,
Now as we part and go our several ways,
Touch every lip, may every voice be praise:

Praise for the fellowship that here we find,
The fellowship of heart and soul and mind,
Praise for the bonds of brother, sisterhood,
Bonds wrought by thee, who makest all things good.

Here has dull care been banished from our thought,
Here has glad fellowship our spirits caught
To heights undreamed of midst the busy maze,
The toil and worry of our working days.

Yet must these come again; for while we wait
High on the mount, in sight of heaven's gate,
Breaks there upon our ears the sound of strife,
The noise and clamour of our daily life.

Lord, make us strong, for thou alone dost know
How oft we turn our faces from the foe;
How oft, when claimed by dark temptation's hour,
We lose our hold of thee, and of thy power.

Go with us, Lord, from hence; we only ask
That thou be sharer in our daily task;
So, side by side with thee, shall each one know
The blessedness of heaven begun below.

*W. V. Jenkins**

468

Angel's Song L.M.

FORTH in thy name, O Lord, I go,
My daily labour to pursue;
Thee, only thee, resolved to know,
In all I think or speak, or do.

The task thy wisdom hath assigned
O let me cheerfully fulfil;
In all my works thy presence find,
And prove thine acceptable will.

Thee may I set at my right hand,
Whose eyes mine inmost spirit see;
And labour on at thy command,
And offer all my works to thee.

Give me to bear thy easy yoke,
And every moment watch and pray,
And still to things eternal look,
And hasten to thy glorious day:

For thee delightfully employ
Whate'er thy bounteous grace hath given,
And run my course with even joy,
And closely walk with thee to heaven.

Charles Wesley

469

Southwell C.M.

NOT on this day, O God, alone
 Would we thy presence seek,
But find its hallowing power our own
 Through all the coming week.

If calm and bright its moments prove,
 Untouched by pain or woe,
May they reflect a thankful love
 To thee, from whom they flow.

Or should they bring us griefs severe,
 Still may we lean on thee,
And, though our eyes let fall the tear,
 At peace our spirits be.

In every scene, or dark, or bright,
 Thy favour may we seek;
And O do thou direct us right
 Through all the coming week!

*W. Gaskell**

470

Mannheim 87.87.87.

LORD, dismiss us with thy blessing;
 Fill our hearts with joy and peace;
Let us each, thy love possessing,
 Still in holiness increase;
  O sustain us,
 Till the day of conflict cease!

Thanks we give and adoration
  For thy gospel's joyful sound;
May the fruits of thy salvation
  In our hearts and lives abound.
    May thy presence
  With us evermore be found!

*J. Fawcett**

471

Randolph 9.88.9.

GOD be with you till we meet again;
  May he through the days direct you;
  May he in life's storms protect you;
God be with you till we meet again.

God be with you till we meet again;
  And when doubts and fears oppress you,
  May his holy peace possess you;
God be with you till we meet again.

God be with you till we meet again;
  In distress his grace sustain you;
  In success from pride restrain you;
God be with you till we meet again.

God be with you till we meet again;
  May he go through life beside you,
  And through death in safety guide you;
God be with you till we meet again.

Donald Hughes, based on J. E. Rankin

472

Tallis' Ordinal C.M.

ETERNAL Life, whose love divine
  Enfolds us each and all,
We know no other truth than thine,
  We heed no other call.

Oh, may we serve in thought and deed
  Thy kingdom yet to be,
Till Truth and Righteousness and Love
  Shall lead all souls to thee!

Emma E. Marean

473

God be in my head   Irregular

GOD be in my head,
  And in my understanding;
God be in mine eyes,
  And in my looking;
God be in my mouth,
  And in my speaking;
God be in my heart,
  And in my thinking;
God be at mine end,
  And at my departing.

Sarum Primer

474

Melcombe   L.M.

FROM all that dwell below the skies
Let faith and hope with love arise;
Let beauty, truth and good be sung
Through every land, by every tongue.

475

Tallis' Canon   L.M.

PRAISE God for Love we all may share;
Praise God for Beauty everywhere;
Praise God for Hope of Good to be;
Praise God for Truth that makes us free.

476

Old 100th   L.M.

PRAISE God, from whom all blessings flow;
Praise him, all creatures here below;
Praise him, ye heavenly hosts above;
Praise him, my soul, for all his love.

Index of First Lines and Tune Sources

Key to abbreviations

HWR	*Hymns of Worship Revised*	†	HWR alternative tune also recommended
HW	*Hymns of Worship*	MS	New hymn – tune available in manuscript
HL	*Hymns for Living*	WOV	*With One Voice* (Collins 1979)
H/Psms	*Hymns and Psalms* (Methodist Publishing House)	HCL	*Hymns for the Celebration of Life*
SOP	*Songs of Praise*		
BR	*Bristol Tune Book*		

INDEX OF FIRST LINES AND TUNE SOURCES

INDEX OF FIRST LINES AND TUNE SOURCES

INDEX OF FIRST LINES AND TUNE SOURCES

INDEX OF FIRST LINES AND TUNE SOURCES

Index of Themes

This index is arranged in sections as follows:

Hymns which are of *special relevance* to any particular theme have a number with an asterisk.
There is *cross-referencing*: (i) within each section, (ii) between sections and (iii) to the contents sections of the hymn book. The cross-referencing within each section is self-evident; the other cross-references are clearly indicated.

GOD

JESUS CHRIST

THE HOLY SPIRIT OF GOD

THE CHURCH (UNIVERSAL AND LOCAL)

THE CHURCH'S YEAR

CHRISTIAN WORSHIP

THE BIBLE (*References to proper names*)

CHRISTIAN LIFE

INDEX OF THEMES

Index of Authors
Translators and Sources

(with brief items of biographical or other information)